"TREASURE"

Bible Concordance For Elementary Christians

Dave Coleman
"QTMC Dad"

Cover Design by Dave Coleman
Cover Created by Rayfus Jones
Photo of Dave Coleman by Angelo Gibson
Photo of CENTERSTAGE Building by Dave Coleman
Scripture taken from the King James Version of the Bible

WestBow Press books may be ordered through booksellers or by contacting:

WestBow Press
A Division of Thomas Nelson & Zondervan
1663 Liberty Drive
Bloomington, IN 47403
www.westbowpress.com
1 (866) 928-1240

ISBN: 978-1-5127-3733-2 (sc)
ISBN: 978-1-5127-3734-9 (hc)
ISBN: 978-1-5127-3732-5 (e)

Library of Congress Control Number: 2016905832

Print information available on the last page.

WestBow Press rev. date: 07/13/2016

This comprehensive wealth of consolidated scriptures is your *"treasure"*. The Bible is a Parable and a puzzle, and requires wisdom to discern where all the pieces fit together. The path to Heaven is a challenging journey, and every day in our lives, situations arise which call for the Christian response. Christians strive to gain wisdom in the will of God, in order to keep ourselves worthy to do God's will, and to receive His favor. We're commanded to meditate, diligently study, and to always be ready to give an answer. My delight is in the law of the Lord; and in His law do I strive to meditate day and night. Read and familiarize yourself with this book so that you can quickly refer to it as your personal concordance for guidance to popular scriptures and stories which support your Biblical answers as it strengthens you in your spiritual growth, and helps mold Christian values and character. Excerpts are shown in many cases in this book, so make sure to read your Bible's complete associated scriptures for yourself in order to get further understanding.

Each featured topic includes randomly related scriptures, so this book may not be complete with *all* scriptures in the Bible about that subject; this is merely a starting point to answer "where can I find *any* scriptures about this topic in the Bible?" The Bible emphasizes many topics repetitiously, in order to magnify their importance in our Christian growth. We're *all* elementary Christians.

One fellow told me that I am a "gangster for God", and that I "go hard in the paint" (he must be a basketball fan). As the Director of the QTMC Charity Homeless Shelter at the CENTERSTAGE building in Pontiac, Michigan, I have developed 19 years of experience with the Homeless and developmentally challenged community. This is "ground-zero" boot camp for what it takes to be a Christian, and we are the face of hope as we open our facilities to provide refuge to persons less fortunate. God has uniquely positioned us in this environment, at this time, and filled me with the knowledge and experience to confidently encourage others who may be serious about their spiritual growth and walk with God.

This book presumes that the reader has already made the most important decision of their spiritual life and accepted Jesus Christ as their savior, yet provides a level of comfort to help others make that decision. Too many people are in denial and think that they will be able to reach Heaven based solely upon the thousands of flamboyant sermons that they have heard over their lifetime; but please don't get it twisted. It's going to take righteous judgment, plus a sincere balance of prayer, fasting, alms, faith, praise, worship, works, dedication, sacrifice, wisdom, forgiveness, refrain, biblical study, tithing, and much more, to diligently strive to achieve the righteousness of a saint. Wouldn't it be a surprise if you missed Heaven by *this* much because you neglected the importance of studying the Bible for yourself, and you trusted your soul and salvation to other people's wrong opinions, instead of reading these scriptures and getting the facts for yourself?

This book emphasizes the importance of "works". We should all consider what we have done for Him lately. Wherever sacrifices are made, there are blessings in store. We simply **must** do works. I've noticed that many people are not concerned about the consequences of their actions, and are not afraid of the Lake of Fire. This book was written for those of us who are.

Table of Contents

vi

About The Author

Dave Coleman is 66 years old, has been married for 48 years to the same bride, raised 4 children and 9 grandchildren, and has resided in Pontiac, Michigan for the last 31 years since moving from Charlotte, NC. He retired in Fleet Sales after 40 years with General Motors.

He is a member of Trinity Missionary Baptist Church for 30 years, accepted Jesus Christ as his savior on June 30, 1988, and has become increasingly more active in missionary work serving the community since 1997. He has experienced tremendous spiritual growth through prayer vigils and guidance of the Pastors, plus "Sweet Hour of Prayer" bible study which he conducts at his Homeless / Special Needs shelter.

He is the Manager for 30 years of QTMC Music Group, which has performed more than 1,200 dynamic motivational concerts at countless locations for millions of youth. He has written or co-written 33 songs performed by QTMC, so concerts include songs from 4 CDs he produced: "Positive Influences", "Mission Possible", "Empowered", and "Change The World". Go to YouTube, then the playlist named "QTMC & CENTERSTAGE & Harlem Globetrotters" to view about 30 videos.

He and QTMC visits children and have delivered toys to rehabilitating youth at St. Joseph Hospital, Mercy Place Hospital, and Doctor's Hospital Europeds at Christmas time for 12 years.

He is the author of 4 books: "The Man Who Could See Angels", "Read To Succeed", "A Special Place in God's Heart", and "Treasure".

He hosts a dinner dance twice a month for developmentally challenged adult "Special Needs" persons, complete with dress-up "Prom Dance" in May and "Homecoming Dance" in October for the last 5 years.

He hosts an annual Memorial Day Picnic for Veterans and the entire community, complete with buffet, family games, and BounceHouse.

He routinely visits and ministers to homeless individuals as well as women's groups incarcerated at Oakland County Jail in Pontiac, Michigan.

He is the Case Manager for developing Third Party Homeless Verification Letters to local housing and support agencies.

He obtains emergency blankets from the federal government program and donates them to homeless/needy persons and shares them with other local support agencies.

He distributes thousands of pounds of USDA food (average 12 pallets) to the community every week, from networking with Forgotten Harvest, Gleaners Food Bank, Whole Foods Market, Lutheran Church, and others.

He collaborates in April and October for 13 years with the local animal care networks to host dog & cat Shot Vaccination Clinics by licensed veterinarians and immunized thousands of animals.

His favorite hobby is 9-ball billiards. He plays in a 16-member league competition at Main Street Billiards in Rochester, Michigan. In 2009, he won 1st place championship, and ranks close to the top every year. His moniker is "Air Force-1" because he expects the same winning result regardless of cue stick that he shoots with.

He is the Vehicles Coordinator & Music Engineer for the Pontiac Parade Extravaganza for the last 11 years (see Santa's microphones).

He is the President/Chairman/Director for 19 years of CENTERSTAGE Rental Hall/Recording Studio, CSTAGE Music & Book Publishing Co. and QTMC, Inc. Charity & Homeless Shelter, where he has served thousands of nutritious balanced buffet meals, plus taken Homeless / Special Needs persons to Auto Shows and Pistons Games, Shows, and concerts.

He is a person of stability, strong family values, and integrity. As evidenced by the prestigious commendations shown below, he is diligent to perform as many "works" as he can as he strives to be God's servant.

He considers himself bountifully blessed and that he receives God's favor in scriptures like: **1-Corinthians 2:9 Eyes have not seen**, ears haven't heard, and neither has it entered into the hearts of those, the things which God hath prepared for them who love Him. **Psalm 84:11** The Lord will give grace and glory: **no good thing will He withhold from them that walk uprightly. Hebrews 11:6** But without faith it is impossible to please Him: for he that cometh to God must believe that He is, and that **He is a rewarder of them that diligently seek Him.**

Please welcome....... Dave "QTMC Dad" Coleman !!

For his accomplishments and community involvement, Dave Coleman has proudly received distinguished awards including:

- General Motors "Civic Spirit Award" 1995.
- Student Leadership Services "Lifetime Achievement Award" 2000.
- NFL Detroit Lions "Community Quarterback Award" 2001.
- Michigan Recreation & Park Association "MRPA Award" 2002.
- Winter Olympics "Olympic Torchbearer Award" 2002.
- Alpha Kappa Alpha Sorority "Community Service Award" 2006.
- Pontiac Parade Extravaganza MVP "ANGEL Award" 2006.
- Army Garrison-Detroit Arsenal "Alcohol Awareness Award" 2007.
- T&C Credit U. "Woodward 200th Birthday/Cleanup Award" 2007.
- Alpha Kappa Alpha Sorority "Humanitarian Award" 2008.
- Boy Scouts of America "Pontiac Achievers Award" 2009.
- Cousino Care Conference "Caregiver Of The Year Award" 2009.
- Rochester, MI "1st Place Billiards Champion: Air Force-1" 2009.
- Zeta Phi Beta Sorority "Family of The Year Award" 2010.
- City/Pontiac Mayor Phillips "Mayoral Proclamation Award" 2010.
- Congressman Peters "Cert. Special Recognition Award" 2010.
- Governor Granholm "State of MI. Cert. of Tribute Award" 2010.
- State Rep. Melton "State of MI. Special Tribute Award" 2010.
- Oakland Co. Exec. Patterson "Cty Exec. Declaration Award" 2010.
- Oak. Co. Bd Com. Greimel/Hatchett "Proclamation Award" 2010.
- Pont. Council Jones/Waterman "Cert. Recognition Award" 2010.
- City of Pontiac Mayor Jukowski "Cert. Recognition Award" 2010.
- MBTA "Michigan Business Travel Association Award" 2011.
- Michigan State Association "ELKS 85th Convention Award" 2011.
- New Experience "Spirit Pontiac Servant Leadership Award" 2011.
- NBA Detroit Pistons "Game Changer Award" 2012.
- Pontiac Regional Chamber "All-Star Award" 2012.
- Thompson Brothers awarded 1980 25-ft SeaRay Cabin Boat 2012.
- Oakland Press Newspaper "Unsung Hero Award" 2013.
- Pontiac Downtown Business Association "Senior Award" 2013.
- Clyde's Frame/Wheel awarded new 20-ft CargoMate Trailer 2014.
- Whole Foods Market awarded used Pallet Jack to load trailer 2014.
- Wayne State Univ. Honorary "Golden Key Honour Society" 2014.
- American Legion Post 377 Veterans awarded new USA flag 2015.
- Corporate Auto awarded new Chevy Silverado Pickup Truck 2016.
- Notary Public, Oakland County, Michigan 2014 - 2020.

MISSION STATEMENT

"We will live our lives in such a way that those who know us, but don't know Christ, will come to know Christ, because they know us. Therefore, we resolve to be tender with the young, compassionate with the aged, sympathetic with the striving, and tolerant of the weak and the wrong, because at sometime in life, we will have been all of these. We should strive to always practice J-O-Y: Jesus first, Others second, and Yourself last. With an attitude of gratitude, let's gratefully approach every day expecting miracles, blessings, and Angels, as we strive to keep ourselves worthy to do God's will. We're going to do all that we can, and then stand back and let the Master do all that we can't. We shall forever endeavor to fight the good fight for those who seem to have a special place in God's heart by providing food, clothing, or shelter relief to persons who are poor, homeless, needy, maimed, lame, blind, imprisoned, sick, afflicted, widows, fatherless, or Special Needs, and to treat them with love, dignity, compassion, and respect. We don't know what the future holds, but we know who holds the future."

Dave Coleman, Servant.

Matthew 6:19-21 Lay not up for yourselves **treasures** upon earth, where moth and rust doth corrupt, and where thieves break through and steal: But lay up for yourselves **treasures** in Heaven, where neither moth nor rust doth corrupt, and where thieves do not break through nor steal: For where your **treasure** is, there will your heart be also.

Matthew 19:21 Jesus said to him, If you want to be perfect, go, sell what you have and **give to the poor, and you will have treasure in Heaven**; and come, follow Me.

Mark 10:21 Then Jesus, looking at him, loved him, and said to him, One thing you lack: Go your way, sell whatever you have and **give to the poor, and you will have treasure in Heaven**; and come, take up the cross, and follow Me.

Luke 18:22 So when Jesus heard these things, He said to him, you still lack one thing. Sell all that you have and **distribute to the poor, and you will have treasure in Heaven**; and come, follow Me.

1-Corinthians 13:1-8, 13 Though I speak with the tongues of men and of Angels, and have not charity (love), I am become as sounding brass, or a tinkling cymbal. And though I have the gift of prophecy, and understand all mysteries, and all knowledge; and though I have all faith, so that I could remove mountains, and have not charity (love), I am nothing. And though I bestow all my goods to feed the poor, and though I give my body to be burned, and have not charity (love), it profiteth me nothing. Charity (love) suffereth long, and is kind; charity (love) envieth not; charity (love) vaunteth not itself, is not puffed up, Doth not behave itself unseemly, seeketh not her own, is not easily provoked, thinketh no evil; Rejoiceth not in iniquity, but rejoiceth in the truth; Beareth all things, believeth all things, hopeth all things, endureth all things. Charity (love) never faileth: And now abideth faith, hope, Charity (love), these three; but the greatest of these is Charity (love).

1

"Works" Regarding Persons Poor, Homeless (Jesus Was Homeless), Needy, Maimed, Lame, Deaf, Dumb, Blind, Afflicted, Sick, Weak, Aliens, Imprisoned, Widows, Fatherless (Those Who Seem To Have A Special Place In God's Heart); The Man Born Blind

Doing **"works"** is extremely important, yet its importance has been overlooked for far too many years, and is seldom talked or preached about. As I researched the scriptures in preparation for this book, it is reiterated several times that **we all will be "judged according to our works".** Then I started to realize that if people don't know how important that it is, they may not know that they need to be doing more. We all have heard that "faith without works is dead." **(James 2:26)**

I was the keynote speaker in February 2015 at a church during Black History Month for their youth day. So I put the young folk to the challenge by reading scriptures regarding "judged according to our works", then I asked them to reply with the interpretation/definition of "works" and to give me some examples. Everyone flunked the question, and my inquiry elicited uncertainty even from the rest of the congregation and adults. That inspired me that I should emphasize the importance of "works" even more to everyone who comes within the sound of my voice, or within reading of this book.

As indicated by the upcoming scriptures, one day we will be "judged according to our works". That should compel each of us to ask ourselves questions such as, "What does it mean, that I will be judged, if I've already made it into Heaven?", "What are works?", plus "Who should I do works for?" Let's analyze these three questions:

The dictionary definition of _judge_ includes: "to pass judgment on, or to sentence; to decide or deem something after inquiry or deliberation; or, to appraise something or somebody critically." Considering these, persons seeking Heaven may interpret this in either of two ways: that

2

"judged" means whether you will even get to Heaven or you may have fallen short and will go to Hell, or that "judged" means that within Heaven, somebody will be closer to Jesus than others. Some people treat their salvation like they want to do only enough to barely get into Heaven, remaining so close to the line that they could just as easily slip into Hell, whereas some of us are very sincere about our standing with God, and whether or not we are doing those things which will keep us in the center of His will and ensure our closeness to Jesus in the Kingdom of Heaven. I'm trying to do all the works that I can in order to get as close as I can to Jesus. He has equipped me to be a champion for the Kingdom.

The dictionary definition of *works* includes: "The deeds of a person, especially virtuous or moral deeds performed as religious acts, for example works of charity."

The following scripture in particular emphasizes that **works should be done without expecting reciprocation in return. Luke 14:12-13, 21** When thou makest a dinner or a supper, call not thy friends, nor thy brethren, neither thy kinsmen, nor thy rich neighbors; lest they also bid thee again, and a recompense be made thee. But when thou makest a feast, call the **poor**, the **maimed**, the **lame**, and the **blind**: **and thou shalt be blessed; for they cannot recompense thee:** for thou shalt be recompensed at the resurrection of the just. So that servant came and reported these things to his master. Then the master of the house, being angry, said to his servant, Go out quickly into the streets and lanes of the city, bring in here the **poor** and the **maimed** and the **lame** and the **blind**.

Matthew 6:1-4 Take heed that ye do not your alms before men, to be seen of them: otherwise ye have no reward of your Father which is in Heaven. Therefore when thou doest thine alms, do not sound a trumpet before thee, as the hypocrites do in the synagogues and in the streets, that they may have glory of men. Verily I say unto you, they have their reward. But when thou doest alms, let not thy left hand know what thy right hand doeth: **That**

3

thine alms may be in secret: and thy Father which seeth in secret Himself shall reward thee openly.

Who should I do works for? Beginning with the groups specified in Luke 14 (poor/homeless, maimed, lame, blind), a search of the internet Bible will guide us to other groups such as needy, deaf, dumb, afflicted, sick, weak, aliens, imprisoned, widows, and fatherless. I've determined that these groups seem to have a special place in God's heart. It seems like He always cares for the underdog. As Director of QTMC, Inc. Charity / CENTERSTAGE Homeless Shelter for 18 years, I have been extremely, extremely surprised at the numerous times that I've been criticized, ostracized, verbalized, brutalized, vilified, and condemned at people's contempt and disdain for helping the homeless. More so than murderers, thieves, or other criminals, homeless people seem to be treated as the most hated group in America. Once I realized though that I was helping people just like Jesus (who was homeless), I resolved to the fact that I'm on the right path, and perhaps everyone else may be on the wrong path. Whenever works are performed / alms are done / sacrifices made, for Christ's sake, blessings arc in store for you and your family.

Luke 9:58 And Jesus said unto him, Foxes have holes, and birds of the air have nests; but the Son of man hath not where to lay His head.

Matthew 8:20 And Jesus saith unto him, The foxes have holes, and the birds of the air have nests; but the Son of man hath not where to lay His head. (Note that **JESUS WAS HOMELESS.**)

Galatians 6:2, 9 Bear ye one another's burdens, and so fulfill the law of Christ. And let us not be weary in well doing: for in due season we shall reap, if we faint not.

Proverbs 17:5 For whoso mocketh the **poor** reproacheth his maker. (Note that if you apply this scripture to other groups such as homeless, needy, maimed, etc., then it's apparent that to criticize/mistreat any of these groups would be to criticize/mistreat their maker, God.)

4

John 14:10-12 Believest thou not that I am in the Father, and the Father in Me? the words that I speak unto you I speak not of Myself: but the Father that dwelleth in Me, He doeth the **works**. Believe Me that I am in the Father, and the Father in Me: or else **believe Me for the very works' sake.** Verily, verily, I say unto you, He that believeth on Me, the **works** that I do shall he do also; and greater **works** than these shall he do; because I go unto My Father.

Matthew 25:35-36, & 40 Jesus said For I was an hungred, and ye gave Me meat; I was thirsty, and ye gave Me drink; I was a **stranger**, and ye took Me in; naked, and ye clothed Me; I was **sick**, and ye visited Me; I was in **prison**, and ye came unto Me. Verily I say unto you, inasmuch as ye have done it unto one of the least of these my brethren, ye have done it unto Me.

Proverbs 21:13 Whoso stoppeth his ears at the cry of the **poor**, he also shall cry himself, but shall not be heard.

Romans 15:1 We then that are strong ought to bear the infirmities of the **weak**.

Proverbs 16:19 Better it is to be of an humble spirit with the lowly, than to divide the spoil with the proud.

Psalm 82:3-4 Defend the **poor** and **Fatherless**; do justice to the **afflicted** and **needy**. Deliver the **poor** and **needy**; free them from the hand of the wicked.

Hebrews 13:2 Be not forgetful to entertain strangers; **for thereby some have entertained Angels unawares.**

James 1:27 **Pure religion before God is this**: to visit the **Fatherless** and **widows** in their affliction.

Zechariah 7:10 Do not oppress the **widow** or the **Fatherless**, the **alien** or the **poor**. Let none of you plan evil in his heart against his brother.

Proverbs 22:2 The rich and the **poor** meet together, **the Lord is the maker of them all.**

Job 20:10, 19 His children will seek the favor of the **poor**, and his hands will restore his wealth. For he has oppressed and forsaken the **poor**, he has violently seized a house which he did not build.

Deuteronomy 15:7, 11 If there is among you a **poor** man of your brethren, within any of the gates in your land which the Lord your God is giving you, you shall not harden your heart nor shut your hand from your **poor** brother. For the **poor** will never cease from the land; therefore I command you, saying, You shall open your hand wide to your brother, to your **poor** and your **needy**, in your land.

Job 29:12, 16 Because I delivered the **poor** who cried out, the **Fatherless** and the **one who had no helper**. I was a Father to the **poor**, and I searched out the case that I did not know.

Job 36:15 He delivers the **poor** in their affliction, and opens their ears in oppression.

Psalm 107:41 Yet He sets the **poor** on high, far from affliction, and makes their families like a flock.

Psalm 140:12 I know that the Lord will maintain the cause of the **afflicted**, and justice for the **poor**.

Psalm 12:5 For the oppression of the **poor**, for the sighing of the **needy**, now I will arise, says the Lord; I will set him in the safety for which he yearns.

Psalm 69:33 For the Lord hears the **poor**, and does not despise His prisoners.

Psalm 72:12-13 He will bring justice to the **poor** of the people; He will save the children of the **needy**, and will break in pieces the oppressor. For He will deliver the **needy** when he cries, the **poor** also, and **him who has no helper**. He will spare the **poor** and **needy**, and will save the souls of the **needy**.

Psalm 109:31 For He shall stand at the right hand of the **poor**, to save him from those who condemn him.

James 2:2-4 For if there should come into your assembly a man with gold rings, in fine apparel, and there should also come in a **poor** man in filthy clothes, And you pay attention to the one wearing the fine clothes and say to him, You sit here in a good place, and say to the **poor** man, You stand there, or, Sit here at my footstool, Are ye not then partial in yourselves, and are become judges of evil thoughts?

James 2:5 Listen, my beloved brethren: **Has God not chosen the poor of this world to be rich in faith and heirs of the kingdom which He promised to those who love Him?**

Exodus 23:3, 6 You shall not show partiality to a **poor** man in his dispute. You shall not pervert the judgment of your **poor** in his dispute.

Psalm 34:6 This **poor** man cried out, and the Lord heard him, and saved him out of all his troubles.

Deuteronomy 24:12, 14 And if the man is **poor**, you shall not keep his pledge overnight. You shall not oppress a hired servant who is **poor** and **needy**, whether one of your brethren or one of the **aliens** who is in your land within your gates.

1-Samuel 2:7-8 The Lord makes **poor** and makes rich; He brings low and lifts up. He raises the **poor** from the dust and lifts the beggar from the ash heap, to set them among princes, And make them inherit the throne of glory. For the pillars of the earth are the Lord's, and He has set the world upon them.

Psalm 10:2, 9 The wicked in his pride persecutes the **poor**; let them be caught in the plots which they have devised. He lies in wait secretly, as a lion in his den; he lies in wait to catch the **poor**; he catches the **poor** when he draws him into his net.

Job 24:4, 9-10, 14 They push the **needy** off the road; all the **poor** of the land are forced to hide. Some snatch the **Fatherless** from the breast, and take a pledge from the **poor**. They cause the **poor** to go naked, without clothing; and they take away the sheaves from the hungry. The murderer rises with the light; he kills the **poor** and **needy**; and in the night he is like a thief.

Psalm 9:18 For the **needy** shall not always be forgotten; the expectation of the **poor** shall not perish forever.

Job 5:16 So the **poor** have hope, and injustice shuts her mouth.

Job 30:25 Have I not wept for him who was in trouble? Has not my soul grieved for the **poor**?

Job 31:16, 19 If I have kept the **poor** from their desire, or caused the eyes of the **widow** to fail, If I have seen anyone perish for lack of clothing, or any **poor** man without covering;

Job 34:28 So that they caused the cry of the **poor** to come to Him; for He hears the cry of the **afflicted**.

Psalm 22:26 The **poor** shall eat and be satisfied; those who seek Him will praise the Lord. Let your heart live forever!

Psalm 72:2 He will judge your people with righteousness, and your **poor** with justice.

Psalm 68:10 Your congregation dwelt in it; you, O God, provided from Your goodness for the **poor**.

Psalm 70:5 But I am **poor** and **needy**; make haste to me, O God!

Psalm 69:29 But I am **poor** and sorrowful; let Your salvation, O God, set me up on high.

Psalm 74:19, 21 Do not forget the life of your **poor** forever. Let the **poor** and **needy** praise your name.

Psalm 86:1 Bow down your ear, O Lord, hear me; for I am **poor** and **needy**.

Psalm 109:22 For I am **poor** and **needy**, and my heart is wounded within me.

Psalm 112:9 He has dispersed abroad, He has given to the **poor**; His righteousness endures forever; His horn will be exalted with honor.

Psalm 113:7 He raises the **poor** out of the dust, and lifts the **needy** out of the ash heap,

Psalm 132:15 I will abundantly bless her provision; I will satisfy her **poor** with bread.

Proverbs 19:22 What is desired in a man is kindness, and a **poor** man is better than a liar.

Proverbs 10:4, 15 He who has a slack hand becomes **poor**, but the hand of the diligent makes rich. The rich man's wealth is his strong city; the destruction of the **poor** is their poverty.

Proverbs 29:13-14 The **poor** man and the oppressor have this in common: the Lord gives light to the eyes of both. The king who judges the **poor** with truth, his throne will be established forever.

Psalm 35:10 All my bones shall say, Lord, who is like You, delivering the **poor** from him who is too strong for him, yes, the **poor** and the **needy** from him who plunders him?

Proverbs 22:2, 7, 9, 16, 22 The rich and the **poor** have this in common, **the Lord is the maker of them all.** The rich rules over the **poor, and the borrower is servant to the lender.** He who has a generous eye will be blessed, for he gives of his bread to the **poor.** He who oppresses the **poor** to increase his riches, and he who gives to the rich, will surely come to poverty. Do not rob the **poor** because he is **poor**, nor oppress the **afflicted** at the gate;

Proverbs 13:7-8, 23   There is one who makes himself rich, yet has nothing; and one who makes himself **poor**, yet has great riches.   The ransom of a man's life is his riches, but the **poor** does not hear rebuke.   Much food is in the fallow ground of the **poor**, and for lack of justice there is waste.

Proverbs 28:3, 6, 8, 11, 15, 27   A **poor** man who oppresses the **poor** is like a driving rain which leaves no food.   Better is the **poor** who walks in his integrity than one perverse in his ways, though he be rich.   One who increases his possessions by usury and extortion gathers it for him who will pity the **poor**.   The rich man is wise in his own eyes, but the **poor** who has understanding searches him out.   Like a roaring lion and a charging bear is a wicked ruler over **poor** people.   He who gives to the **poor** will not lack, but he who hides his eyes will have many curses.

Proverbs 30:9, 14   Lest I be full and deny you and say, Who is the Lord? or lest I be **poor** and steal, and profane the name of my God.   There is a generation whose teeth are like swords, and whose fangs are like knives, to devour the **poor** from off the earth, and the **needy** from among men.

Ecclesiastes 9:15-16   Now there was found in it a **poor** wise man, and he by his wisdom delivered the city. Yet no one remembered that same **poor** man.   **Wisdom is better than strength.**   Nevertheless the **poor** man's wisdom is despised, and his words are not heard.

Ecclesiastes 4:13-14   Better a **poor** and wise youth than an old and foolish king who will be admonished no more.   For he comes out of prison to be king, although he was born **poor** in his kingdom.

Ecclesiastes 5:8   If you see the oppression of the **poor**, and the violent perversion of justice and righteousness in a province, do not marvel at the matter; for high official watches over high official, ... higher officials are over them.

Ecclesiastes 6:8   For what more has the wise man than the fool?   What does the **poor** man have, who knows how to walk before the living?

Psalm 14:6 You shame the counsel of the **poor**, but the Lord is his refuge.

Isaiah 10:2 To rob the **needy** of justice, and to take what is right from the **poor** of my people, that **widows** may be their prey, and that they may rob the **Fatherless**.

Isaiah 25:4 For you have been a strength to the **poor**, a strength to the **needy** in his distress, a refuge from the storm, a shade from the heat; for the blast of the terrible ones is as a storm against the wall.

Isaiah 11:4 But with righteousness He shall judge the **poor**, and decide with equity for the **meek** of the earth; He shall strike the earth with the rod of His mouth, and with the breath of His lips He shall slay the wicked.

Proverbs 21:17 He who loves pleasure will be a **poor** man; he who loves wine and oil will not be rich.

Isaiah 26:6 The foot shall tread it down - the feet of the **poor** and the steps of the **needy**.

Isaiah 29:19 The humble also shall increase their joy in the Lord, and the **poor** among men shall rejoice in the Holy One of Israel.

Isaiah 32:7 Also the schemes of the schemer are evil; he devises wicked plans to destroy the **poor** with lying words, even when the **needy** speaks justice.

Isaiah 41:17 The **poor** and **needy** seek water, but there is none, their tongues fail for thirst. I, the Lord, will hear them; I, the God of Israel, will not forsake them.

Isaiah 58:7 Is it not to share your bread with the hungry, and that you bring to your house the **poor** who are cast out; when you see the naked, that you cover him, and not hide yourself from your own flesh?

Luke 4:18 The Spirit of the Lord is upon Me, because He has anointed me to preach the gospel to the **poor**;

Daniel 4:27 Therefore, O king, let my advice be acceptable to you; break off your sins by being righteous, and your iniquities by showing mercy to the **poor**. Perhaps there may be a lengthening of your prosperity.

Jeremiah 5:4 Surely these are **poor**. They are foolish; for they do not know the way of the Lord, the judgment of their God.

Jeremiah 20:13 Sing to the Lord! Praise the Lord! For He has delivered the life of the **poor** from the hand of evildoers.

Jeremiah 22:16 He judged the cause of the **poor** and **needy**; then it was well.

Ezekiel 18:12 If he has oppressed the **poor** and **needy**, robbed by violence, not restored the pledge, lifted his eyes to the idols, or committed abomination;

Ezekiel 22:29 The people of the land have used oppressions, committed robbery, and mistreated the **poor** and **needy**; and they wrongfully oppress the stranger.

Amos 8:4, 6 Hear this, you who swallow up the **needy**, and make the **poor** of the land fail, That we may buy the **poor** for silver, and the **needy** for a pair of sandals, even sell the bad wheat?

Zechariah 11:7, 11 So I fed the flock for slaughter, in particular the **poor** of the flock. Thus the **poor** of the flock, who were watching me, knew that it was the word of the Lord.

Matthew 11:5 The **blind** see and the **lame** walk; the lepers are cleansed and the **deaf** hear; the dead are raised up and the **poor** have the gospel preached to them.

Matthew 26:9, 11 For this fragrant oil might have been sold for much and given to the **poor**. For you have the **poor** with you always, but Me you do not have always.

Mark 14:5, 7 For it might have been sold for more than three hundred denarii and given to the **poor**. For you have the **poor** with you always, and whenever you wish you may do them good; but Me you do not have always.

Isaiah 61:1 The Spirit of the Lord God is upon me, because the Lord has anointed me to preach good tidings to the **poor**.

John 12:5-6, 8 Why was this fragrant oil not sold for three hundred denarii and given to the **poor**? This he said not that he cared for the **poor**, but because he was a thief and had the money box and he used to take what was put in it. For the **poor** you have with you always, but Me you do not have always.

John 13:29 For some thought, because Judas had the money box, that Jesus had said to him, Buy those things we need for the feast, or that he should give something to the **poor**.

Luke 7:22 Jesus answered and said to them, Go and tell John the things you have seen and heard: that the **blind** see, the **lame** walk, the lepers are cleansed, the **deaf** hear, the dead are raised, the **poor** have the gospel preached to them.

Luke 21:2-3 And He saw also a certain **poor** widow putting in two mites. Truly I say to you that this **poor** widow has put in more than all.

2-Corinthians 6:10 As sorrowful, yet always rejoicing; as **poor**, yet making many rich; as having nothing, and yet possessing all things.

2-Corinthians 8:9 For you know the grace of our Lord Jesus Christ, that though He was rich, yet for your sakes He became **poor**, that you through His poverty might become rich.

2-Corinthians 9:9 He has dispersed abroad, He has given to the **poor**; His righteousness endures forever.

Deuteronomy 15:9 Beware lest there be a wicked thought in your heart, saying, The seventh year, the year of release, is at hand, and your eye be evil against your **poor** brother and you give him nothing, and he cry out to the Lord against you, and it become sin among you.

Deuteronomy 24:15 Each day you shall give him his wages, and not let the sun go down on it, for he is **poor** and has set his heart on it; lest he cry out against you to the Lord, and it be sin to you.

Galatians 2:10 They desired only that we should remember the **poor**, the very thing which I also was eager to do.

Proverbs 31:8 **Open thy mouth for the dumb** in the cause of all such as are appointed to destruction.

Leviticus 19:14 Thou shalt not curse the **deaf**, nor put a stumblingblock before the **blind**, but shalt fear thy God: I am the LORD.

Matthew 9:32-33 As they went out, behold, they brought to Him a **dumb** man possessed with a devil. And when the devil was cast out, the **dumb** spake: and the multitudes marvelled, saying, It was never so seen in Israel.

Matthew 12:22 Then was brought unto Him one possessed with a devil, **blind**, and **dumb**: and He healed him, insomuch that the **blind** and **dumb** both spake and saw.

Matthew 15:30-31 And great multitudes came unto Him, having with them those that were **lame**, **blind**, **dumb**, **maimed**, and many others, and cast them down at Jesus' feet; and He healed them: Insomuch that the multitude wondered, when they saw the **dumb** to speak, the **maimed** to be whole, the **lame** to walk, and the **blind** to see: and they glorified the God of Israel.

Exodus 4:11 And the LORD said unto him, Who hath made man's mouth? or who maketh the **dumb**, or **deaf**, or the seeing, or the **blind**? have not I the LORD?

Isaiah 29:18 And in that day shall the **deaf** hear the words of the book, and the eyes of the **blind** shall see out of obscurity, and out of darkness.

Mark 7:37 And were beyond measure astonished, saying, He hath done all things well: he maketh both the **deaf** to hear, and the **dumb** to speak.

Isaiah 42:18 Hear, ye **deaf**; and look, ye **blind**, that ye may see.

Isaiah 66:2 For all those things My hand has made, and all those things exist, says the Lord. **But on this one will I look:** On him who is **poor** and of a contrite spirit, and who trembles at My word.

John 9:1-7 And as Jesus passed by, He saw a man which was blind from his birth. And His disciples asked Him, saying, Master, who did sin, this man, or his parents, that he was born blind? Jesus answered, Neither hath this man sinned, nor his parents: but that the **works of God** should be made manifest in him. **I must work the works of Him that sent me, while it is day: the night cometh, when no man can work.** As long as I am in the world, I am the light of the world. When He had thus spoken, He spat on the ground, and made clay of the spittle, and He anointed the eyes of the blind man with the clay, and said unto him, Go, wash in the pool of Siloam. He went his way therefore, and washed, and came seeing.

15

Now that you've been apprised of the importance of "works", you may be wondering what "works" you may consider regarding groups that we're commanded to have compassion for. Here are some suggestions:

Spend time with fatherless kids or orphans.
Drive maimed, lame, blind persons to doctor appointments.
Cut grass for disabled, elderly, or widows.
Help stranded motorists get out of dangerous traffic.
Sponsor or "adopt" a poor needy person, family, or widow.
Take Special Needs persons somewhere special.
Take neighborhood kids to a discount movie.
Get clearance to visit or pen pal with those incarcerated.
Donate to wheelchair bound needy, maimed, lame, blind.
Rake the leaves for elderly, disabled, or widow persons.
Volunteer at Gleaners or Forgotten Harvest warehouse.
Read magazines/books for blind, disabled, or sick persons.
Shine shoes, wash vehicle, or run errands for bereaved.
Shovel snow for disabled, elderly, or widows.
Always seek new family/friends to take to church with you.
Donate much needed items to local homeless shelter.
Buy a meal for an obviously-needy poor person.
Visit persons sick/shut-in at hospitals or at homes.
Volunteer to serve meals at a shelter or soup kitchen.
Organize or attend prayer vigils and invite others also.
Whenever possible, do alms and works in secret.
Donate clothes, shoes, and books to local clothes closets.

2-Corinthians 5:10 **For we must all appear before the judgment seat of Christ;** that every one may receive the things done in his body, **according to that he hath done, whether it be good or bad.**

John 5:22 For the Father judgeth no man, but hath committed all judgment unto the Son:

Matthew 16:27 For the Son of Man shall come in the glory of His Father with his Angels; and then He shall **reward every man according to his works.**

1-Peter 1:17 The Father, who without respect of persons **judgeth according to every man's work.**

Revelation 2:26 And he that overcometh, and keepeth My **works** unto the end, to him will I give power over the nations:

Revelation 20:12 And I saw the dead, small and great, standing before God, and books were opened. And another book was opened, which is the Book of Life. And the dead were **judged according to their works,** by the things which were written in the books.

Revelation 20:13 The sea gave up the dead who were in it, and Death and Hades delivered up the dead who were in them. And they were **judged, each one according to his works.**

Revelation 22:12 **And, behold, I come quickly; and** My reward is with Me, to give every man according as his work shall be.

17

Proverbs 31:9 Open your mouth, **judge righteously**, and plead the cause of the poor and needy.

1-Corinthians 6:2 Do ye not know that the **saints shall judge the world**? and if the world shall be judged by you, are ye unworthy to judge the smallest matters?

1-Corinthians 6:3 Know ye not that we shall **judge Angels**? how much more things that pertain to this life?

Matthew 7:1-2 Judge not, that ye be not judged. For with what judgment ye judge, ye shall be judged: and with what measure ye mete, it shall be measured to you again.

Matthew 7:5 First cast out the beam out of thine own eye; and then shalt thou see clearly to cast out the mote out of thy brother's eye.

John 8:1-11 Jesus went unto the mount of Olives. And early in the morning He came again into the temple, and all the people came unto Him; and He sat down, and taught them. And the scribes and Pharisees brought unto Him a woman taken in adultery; and when they had set her in the midst, They say unto Him, **Master, this woman was taken in adultery, in the very act. Now Moses in the law commanded us, that such should be stoned: but what sayest thou?** This they said, tempting Him, that they might have to accuse Him. But Jesus stooped down, and with His finger wrote on the ground, as though He heard them not. So when they continued asking Him, **He lifted up Himself, and said unto them, he that is without sin among you, let him first cast a stone at her.** And again He stooped down, and wrote on the ground. And they which heard it, being convicted by their own conscience, went out one by one, beginning at the eldest, even unto the last: and Jesus was left alone, and the woman standing in the midst. When Jesus had lifted up Himself, and saw none but the woman, He said unto her, Woman, where are those thine accusers?

18

hath no man condemned thee? She said, No man, Lord. And Jesus said unto her, Neither do I condemn thee: go, and sin no more.

Leviticus 19:15 **You shall do no injustice in judgment.** You shall not be partial to the **poor**, nor honor the person of the mighty. **In righteousness you shall judge your neighbor.**

Romans 14:10-13 But why dost thou judge thy brother? or why dost thou set at nought thy brother? for we shall all stand before the judgment seat of Christ. For it is written, As I live, saith the Lord, every knee shall bow to me, and every tongue shall confess to God. So then every one of us shall give account of himself to God. Let us not therefore judge one another any more: but judge this rather, that no man put a stumblingblock or an occasion to fall in his brother's way.

1-Corinthians 11:23-32 I have received of the Lord that which also I delivered unto you, that the Lord Jesus the same night in which He was betrayed took bread: And when He had given thanks, He brake it, and said, Take, eat: this is My body, which is broken for you: this do in remembrance of Me. After the same manner also He took the cup, when He had supped, saying, this cup is the new testament in My blood: this do ye, as oft as ye drink it, in remembrance of Me. For as often as ye eat this bread, and drink this cup, ye do shew the Lord's death till He come. Wherefore whosoever shall eat this bread, and drink this cup of the Lord, unworthily, shall be guilty of the body and blood of the Lord. **But let a man examine himself,** and so let him eat of that bread, and drink of that cup. **For he that eateth and drinketh unworthily, eateth and drinketh damnation to himself, not discerning the Lord's body. For this cause many are weak and sickly among you, and many sleep. For if we would judge ourselves, we should not be judged.** But when we are judged, we are chastened of the Lord, that we should not be condemned with the world.

19

As Christians, we aspire to emulate our Savior who we admire, Jesus. One of the attributes that we should therefore master is how to be a servant, like Jesus was. Our conversations, actions, or deeds, should be done with a demeanor of love, humility, humbleness, submissiveness, integrity, sincerity, tenderness, faithfulness, gentleness, passion, compassion, and patience. We must forever endeavor to respond in a Christian manner whenever persecuted for Christ's sake, which we are destined to experience many times. Nevertheless, we must demonstrate compassion and understanding at all times as we imitate Christ's example, and always judge righteously. We must pray for those who spitefully use us or persecute us. As we are inspired to become His humble servants, these characteristics are essential, and allow us to perform many "works". The lifestyle of a servant is a commitment and dedication to Jesus' principles and service in pursuit of the kingdom.

Colossians 3:17, 23-24 And whatsoever ye do in word or deed, do all in the name of the Lord Jesus, giving thanks to God and the Father by Him. **And whatever you do, do it heartily, as to the Lord and not unto men.** Knowing that of the Lord ye shall receive the reward of the inheritance: **for ye serve the Lord Christ**.

Matthew 5:16 **Let your light so shine before men**, that they may see your good **works**, and glorify your Father which is in Heaven.

Isaiah 54:17 **No weapon that is formed against thee shall prosper; and every tongue that shall rise against thee in judgment thou shalt condemn. This is the heritage of the servants of the LORD**, and their righteousness is of me, saith the LORD.

Matthew 25:21 His lord said unto him, **Well done, thou good and faithful servant**: thou hast been faithful over a few things, I will make thee ruler over many things: enter thou into the joy of thy lord.

Genesis 24:14 And let it come to pass, that the damsel to whom I shall say, Let down thy pitcher, I pray thee, that I may drink; and she shall say, Drink, and I will give thy camels drink also: let the same be she that thou hast appointed for **Thy servant Isaac**; and thereby shall I know that Thou hast shewed kindness unto my master.

Genesis 26:24 And the LORD appeared unto him the same night, and said, I am the God of Abraham thy father: fear not, for I am with thee, and will bless thee, and multiply thy seed for **My servant Abraham**'s sake.

Exodus 4:10 And **Moses** said unto the LORD, O my LORD, I am not eloquent, neither heretofore, nor since thou hast spoken unto **Thy servant**: but I am slow of speech, and of a slow tongue.

Exodus 14:31 And Israel saw that great work which the LORD did upon the Egyptians: and the people feared the LORD, and believed the LORD, and **His servant Moses**.

Exodus 32:13 Remember **Abraham, Isaac, and Israel, Thy servants**, to whom Thou swarest by Thine own self, and saidst unto them, I will multiply your seed as the stars of heaven, and all this land that I have spoken of will I give unto your seed, and they shall inherit it for ever.

Exodus 33:11 And the LORD spake unto Moses face to face, as a man speaketh unto his friend. And he turned again into the camp: but **His servant Joshua**, the son of Nun, a young man, departed not out of the tabernacle.

Leviticus 25:55 For unto Me the **children of Israel are servants;** they are **My servants** whom I brought forth out of the land of Egypt: I am the LORD your God.

2-Chronicles 32:16 And his servants spake yet more against the LORD God, and against **His servant Hezekiah**.

Numbers 12:8 With him will I speak mouth to mouth, even apparently, and not in dark speeches; and the similitude of the LORD shall he behold: wherefore then were ye not afraid to speak against **My servant Moses**?

Numbers 11:11 And **Moses** said unto the LORD, Wherefore hast thou afflicted **Thy servant**? and wherefore have I not found favour in Thy sight, that Thou layest the burden of all this people upon me?

Deuteronomy 9:27 Remember **Thy servants, Abraham, Isaac**, and **Jacob**; look not unto the stubbornness of this people, nor to their wickedness, nor to their sin:

Joshua 5:14 And he said, Nay; but as captain of the host of the LORD am I now come. And **Joshua** fell on his face to the earth, and did worship, and said unto Him, What saith my Lord unto **His servant**?

Joshua 1:1-2, 7, 13 Now after the death of **Moses the servant** of the LORD it came to pass, that the LORD spake unto Joshua the son of Nun, Moses' minister, saying, **Moses My servant** is dead; now therefore arise, go over this Jordan, thou, and all this people, unto the land which I do give to them, even to the children of Israel. Only be thou strong and very courageous, that thou mayest observe to do according to all the law, which **Moses My servant** commanded thee: turn not from it to the right hand or to the left, that thou mayest prosper withersoever thou goest. Remember the word which **Moses the servant** of the LORD commanded you, saying, the LORD your God hath given you rest, and hath given you this land.

Joshua 8:31 As **Moses the servant** of the Lord commanded the children of Israel, as it is written in the book of the law of Moses, an altar of whole stones, over which no man hath lift up any iron: and they offered thereon burnt offerings unto the LORD, and sacrificed peace offerings.

2-Kings 21:10 And the LORD spake by **His servants the prophets**,

22

Joshua 9:24   And they answered Joshua, and said, Because it was certainly told thy servants, how that the LORD thy God commanded **His servant Moses** to give you all the land, and to destroy all the inhabitants of the land from before you, therefore we were sore afraid of our lives because of you, and have done this thing.

Joshua 12:6   Them did **Moses the servant** of the Lord and the children of Israel smite: and **Moses the servant** of the LORD gave it for a possession unto the Reubenites, and the Gadites, and the half tribe of Manasseh.

Joshua 24:29   And it came to pass after these things, that **Joshua** the son of Nun, **the servant** of the LORD, died, being an hundred and ten years old.

Joshua 11:12, 15   And all the cities of those kings, and all the kings of them, did Joshua take, and smote them with the edge of the sword, and he utterly destroyed them, as **Moses the servant** of the Lord commanded. As the Lord commanded **Moses His servant**, so did Moses command Joshua, and so did Joshua; he left nothing undone of all that the LORD commanded Moses.

1-Samuel 3:10   And the LORD came, and stood, and called as at other times, Samuel, Samuel Then **Samuel** answered, Speak; for **Thy Servant** heareth.

1-Samuel 23:10   Then said **David**, O LORD God of Israel, **Thy servant** hath certainly heard that Saul seeketh to come to Keilah, to destroy the city for my sake.

2-Samuel 3:18   Now then do it: for the LORD hath spoken of David, saying, By the hand of **My servant David** I will save my people Israel out of the hand of the Philistines, and out of the hand of all their enemies.

Isaiah 45:4   For Jacob My **servant**'s sake, and Israel mine elect, I have even called thee by thy name: I have surnamed thee, though thou hast not known Me.

2-Samuel 7:8, 26 Now therefore so shalt thou say unto **My servant David**, Thus saith the LORD of hosts, I took thee from the sheepcote, from following the sheep, to be ruler over my people, over Israel: And let thy name be magnified for ever, saying, The LORD of hosts is the God over Israel: and let the house of **Thy servant David** be established before thee.

1-Kings 3:6 And Solomon said, Thou hast shewed unto **Thy servant David** my father great mercy, according as he walked before thee in truth, and in righteousness, and in uprightness of heart with thee; and thou hast kept for him this great kindness, that thou hast given him a son to sit on his throne, as it is this day.

1-Kings 18:36 And it came to pass at the time of the offering of the evening sacrifice, that **Elijah** the prophet came near, and said, LORD God of Abraham, Isaac, and of Israel, let it be known this day that thou art God in Israel, and that I am **Thy servant**, and that I have done all these things at thy word.

1-Kings 3:9 Give therefore **Thy servant (Solomon)** an understanding heart to judge Thy people, that I may discern between good and bad: for who is able to judge this Thy so great a people?

2-Kings 9:36 Wherefore they came again, and told him. And he said, This is the word of the Lord, which He spake by **His servant Elijah** the Tishbite, saying, In the portion of Jezreel shall dogs eat the flesh of Jezebel:

2-Kings 10:10 Know now that there shall fall unto the earth nothing of the word of the LORD, which the LORD spake concerning the house of Ahab: for the LORD hath done that which He spake by **His servant Elijah**.

James 1:1 James, a servant of God and of the Lord Jesus Christ, to the twelve tribes which are scattered abroad, greeting.

Isaiah 44:1-2, 21   Yet now hear, O **Jacob My servant**; and Israel, whom I have chosen: Thus saith the LORD that made thee, and formed thee from the womb, which will help thee; Fear not, O **Jacob**, **My servant**; and thou, Jesurun, whom I have chosen.   Remember these, O **Jacob** and **Israel**; for thou art **My servant**: I have formed thee; thou art **My servant**: O Israel, thou shalt not be forgotten of Me.

1-Chronicles 6:49   But Aaron and his sons offered upon the altar of the burnt offering, and on the altar of incense, and were appointed for all the work of the place most holy, and to make an atonement for Israel, according to all that **Moses the servant** of God had commanded.

1-Chronicles 17:25-27   For thou, O my God, hast told **Thy servant (David)** that Thou wilt build him an house: therefore **Thy servant** hath found in his heart to pray before Thee.   And now, LORD, thou art God, and hast promised this goodness unto **Thy servant**: Now therefore let it please Thee to bless the house of **Thy servant**, that it may be before Thee for ever: for Thou blessest, O LORD, and it shall be blessed for ever.

2-Chronicles 1:3   So Solomon, and all the congregation with him, went to the high place that was at Gibeon; for there was the tabernacle of the congregation of God, which **Moses the servant** of the LORD had made in the wilderness.

Isaiah 22:20   And it shall come to pass in that day, that I will call **My servant Eliakim** the son of Hilkiah:

Isaiah 41:8   But thou, **Israel**, art my servant , Jacob whom I have chosen, the seed of Abraham my friend.

Isaiah 48:20   Go ye forth of Babylon, flee ye from the Chaldeans, with a voice of singing declare ye, tell this, utter it even to the end of the earth; say ye, The LORD hath redeemed **His servant Jacob**.

25

Isaiah 49:5 And now, saith the LORD that formed me from the womb to be **His servant (Isaiah)**, to bring Jacob again to him, Though Israel be not gathered, yet shall I be glorious in the eyes of the LORD, and my God shall be my strength.

Jeremiah 30:10 Therefore fear thou not, O **My servant Jacob**, saith the LORD; neither be dismayed, O Israel: for, lo, I will save thee from afar, and thy seed from the land of their captivity; and Jacob shall return, and shall be in rest, and be quiet, and none shall make him afraid.

Jeremiah 46:28 Fear thou not, O **Jacob My servant**, saith the LORD: for I am with thee; for I will make a full end of all the nations whither I have driven thee: but I will not make a full end of thee, but correct thee in measure; yet will I not leave thee wholly unpunished.

Jeremiah 25:9 Behold, I will send and take all the families of the north, saith the LORD, and **Nebuchadrezzar** the king of Babylon, **My servant**, and will bring them against this land, and against the inhabitants thereof, and against all these nations round about, and will utterly destroy them, and make them an astonishment, and an hissing, and perpetual desolations.

Jeremiah 33:26 Then will I cast away the seed of Jacob and **David My servant**, so that I will not take any of his seed to be rulers over the seed of Abraham, Isaac, and Jacob: for I will cause their captivity to return, and have mercy on them.

Jude 1:1 **Jude, the servant** of Jesus Christ, and brother of James, to them that are sanctified by God the Father, and preserved in Jesus Christ, and called:

Ezekiel 28:25 Thus saith the Lord GOD; When I shall have gathered the house of Israel from the people among whom they are scattered, and shall be sanctified in them in the sight of the heathen, then shall they dwell in their land that I have given to **My servant Jacob**.

Ezekiel 37:25 And they shall dwell in the land that I have given unto **Jacob My servant**, wherein your fathers have dwelt; and they shall dwell therein, even they, and their children, and their children's children for ever: and **My servant David** shall be their prince for ever.

Job 42:7-8 And it was so, that after the LORD had spoken these words unto Job, the LORD said to Eliphaz the Temanite, My wrath is kindled against thee, and against thy two friends: for ye have not spoken of Me the thing that is right, as **My servant Job** hath. Therefore take unto you now seven bullocks and seven rams, and go to **My servant Job**, and offer up for yourselves a burnt offering; and **My servant Job** shall pray for you: for him will I accept: lest I deal with you after your folly, in that ye have not spoken of Me the thing which is right, like **My servant Job**.

Job 2:3 And the LORD said unto Satan, Hast thou considered **My servant Job**, that there is none like him in the earth, a perfect and an upright man, one that feareth God, and escheweth evil? and still he holdeth fast his integrity, although thou movedst Me against him, to destroy him without cause.

Daniel 6:20 And when he came to the den, he cried with a lamentable voice unto Daniel: and the king spake and said to Daniel, O **Daniel**, **servant** of the living God, is thy God, whom thou servest continually, able to deliver thee from the lions?

Daniel 3:26, 28 Then Nebuchadnezzar came near to the mouth of the burning fiery furnace, and spake, and said, **Shadrach**, **Meshach**, and **Abednego**, ye **servants** of the most high God, come forth, and come hither. Then Shadrach, Meshach, and Abednego, came forth of the midst of the fire. Then Nebuchadnezzar spake, and said, Blessed be the God of **Shadrach**, **Meshach**, and **Abednego**, who hath sent his angel, and delivered **His servants** that trusted in him, and have changed the king's word, and yielded their bodies, that they might not serve nor worship any god, except their own God.

Psalm 105:6, 42 O ye seed of **Abraham His servant**, ye children of Jacob his chosen. For he remembered his holy promise, and **Abraham His servant**.

Psalm 119:125, 135 I am **Thy servant**; give me **(David)** understanding, that I may know Thy testimonies. Make Thy face to shine upon **Thy servant**; and teach me Thy statutes.

Haggai 2:23 In that day, saith the LORD of hosts, will I take thee, O **Zerubbabel, My servant**, the son of Shealtiel, saith the LORD, and will make thee as a signet: for I have chosen thee, saith the LORD of hosts.

Philippians 1:1 **Paul** and **Timotheus**, the **servants** of Jesus Christ, to all the saints in Christ Jesus which are at Philippi, with the bishops and deacons:

Philippians 2:7 But made Himself **(Jesus)** of no reputation, and took upon Him the form of a **servant**, and was made in the likeness of men:

Colossians 4:12 **Epaphras**, who is one of you, **a servant** of Christ, saluteth you, always labouring fervently for you in prayers, that ye may stand perfect and complete in all the will of God.

2-Peter 1:1 **Simon Peter, a servant** and an apostle of Jesus Christ, to them that have obtained like precious faith with us through the righteousness of God and our Saviour Jesus Christ:

Revelation 1:1 The Revelation of Jesus Christ, which God gave unto Him, to shew unto **His servants** things which must shortly come to pass; and He sent and signified it by His angel unto **His servant John**:

Matthew 5:44 But I say to you, love your enemies, bless those who curse you, do good to those who hate you, and pray for those who **spitefully use you** and persecute you,

Luke 6:28 Bless those who curse you, and pray for those who **spitefully use you**.

Romans 12:14 Bless them which persecute you: **bless, and curse not.**

Matthew 18:15-17 Moreover if thy brother shall **trespass** against thee, **go and tell him his fault between thee and him alone**: if he shall hear thee, thou hast gained thy brother. But if he will not hear thee, then take with thee one or two more, that in the mouth of two or three witnesses every word may be established. And if he shall neglect to hear them, tell it unto the church: but if he neglect to hear the church, let him be unto thee as an heathen man and a publican.

2-Timothy 3:12 All that live Godly in Jesus shall suffer persecution.

1-Corinthians 4:10 We are fools for Christ's sake.

Romans 8:36 As it is written: For Your sake we are killed all day long; We are accounted as sheep for the slaughter.

Psalm 44:22 As it is written: For Your sake we are killed all day long; We are accounted as sheep for the slaughter.

Proverbs 16:7 When a man's ways please the Lord, he maketh even his enemies to be at peace with him.

1-Peter 3:17 For it is better, if the will of God be so, that we suffer for well doing, than for evil doing.

Matthew 5:10 Blessed are they which are persecuted for righteousness' sake: for theirs is the kingdom of Heaven.

Matthew 5:11 Blessed are ye, when men shall revile you, and persecute you, and shall say all manner of evil against you falsely, for My sake.

Luke 6:22 Blessed are ye, when men shall hate you, and when they shall separate you from their company, and shall reproach you, and cast out your name as evil, for the Son of man's sake.

Romans 12:17-21 **Recompense to no man evil for evil.** Provide things honest in the sight of all men. **If it be possible, as much as lieth in you, live peaceably with all men.** Dearly beloved, avenge not yourselves, but rather give place unto wrath: for it is written, **Vengeance is mine; I will repay, saith the Lord. Therefore if thine enemy hunger, feed him; if he thirst, give him drink: for in so doing thou shalt heap coals of fire on his head. Be not overcome of evil, but overcome evil with good.**

Ecclesiastes 5:1 **Keep thy foot when thou goest to the house of God**, and be more ready to hear, than to give the sacrifice of fools: for they consider not that they do evil.

Romans 10:9, 13 **That if thou shalt confess with thy mouth the Lord Jesus, and shalt believe in thine heart that God hath raised Him from the dead. thou shalt be saved.** For whosoever shall call upon the name of the Lord shall be saved.

Hebrews 10:24-25 And let us consider one another to provoke unto love and to good works: **Not forsaking the assembling of ourselves together,** as the manner of some ..

Isaiah 58:13-14 **If thou turn away thy foot** from the Sabbath, **from doing thy pleasure on My holy day;** and call the Sabbath a delight, the holy of the LORD, honourable; and shalt honour Him, not doing thine own ways, nor finding thine own pleasure, nor speaking thine own words: Then shalt thou delight thyself in the LORD; and I will cause thee to ride upon the high places of the earth, ...

Mark 2:27-28 And He said unto them, The Sabbath was made for man, and not man for the Sabbath: Therefore the Son of man is Lord also of the Sabbath.

Luke 15:4-7, 10 What man of you, having an hundred sheep, if he lose one of them, doth not leave the ninety and nine in the wilderness, and go after that which is lost, until he find it? And when he hath found it, he layeth it on his shoulders, rejoicing. And when he cometh home, he calleth together his friends and neighbours, saying unto them, Rejoice with me; for I have found my sheep which was lost. I say unto you, that likewise joy shall be in Heaven over one sinner that repenteth, more than over ninety and nine just persons, which need no repentance. **There is joy in the presence of the Angels of God over one sinner that repenteth.**

31

<u>Matthew 6:1-4</u> Take heed that ye do not your alms before men, to be seen of them: otherwise ye have no reward of your Father which is in Heaven. Therefore when thou doest thine alms, do not sound a trumpet before thee, as the hypocrites do in the synagogues and in the streets, that they may have glory of men. Verily I say unto you, they have their reward. But when thou doest **alms**, let not thy left hand know what thy right hand doeth: **That thine alms may be in secret: and thy Father which seeth in secret Himself shall reward thee openly.**

<u>Matthew 6:6</u> But thou, when thou **prayest**, enter into thy closet, and when thou hast shut thy door, **pray to thy Father which is in secret; and thy Father which seeth in secret shall reward thee openly.**

<u>Matthew 6:17-18</u> But thou, when thou **fastest**, anoint thine head, and wash thy face; That thou appear not unto men to fast, but unto thy Father which is in secret: **and thy Father, which seeth in secret, shall reward thee openly.**

<u>Mark 9:25-27</u> When Jesus saw that the people came running together, He rebuked the foul spirit. <u>Matthew 17:19-21</u> Then came the disciples to Jesus apart, and said, Why could not we cast him out? And Jesus said unto them, because of your unbelief: for verily I say unto you, If ye have faith as a grain of mustard seed, ye shall say unto this mountain, remove hence to yonder place; and it shall remove; and nothing shall be impossible unto you. **Howbeit this kind goeth not out but by prayer and fasting.**

Philippians 4:6 Do not be anxious about anything, but in everything by **prayer** and supplication with thanksgiving let your requests be made known to God.

James 5:16 Confess your faults one to another, and **pray** one for another, that ye may be healed. The effectual fervent **prayer** of a righteous man availeth much.

1-Thessalonians 5:16-18 Rejoice always, **pray** without ceasing, give thanks in all circumstances; this is the will of God in Christ Jesus for you.

Romans 12:12 Rejoice in hope, be patient in tribulation, be constant in **prayer**.

Ephesians 6:18 Praying at all times in the Spirit, with all prayer and supplication.

1-Timothy 2:8-10 I will therefore that men **pray** everywhere, lifting up holy hands, without wrath and doubting. In like manner also, that women adorn themselves in modest apparel, with shamefacedness and sobriety; not with broided hair, or gold, or pearls, or costly array; But (which becometh women professing godliness) with good works.

Matthew 21:22 And all things, whatsoever ye shall ask in **prayer**, believing, ye shall receive.

John 14:13 Whatever you ask in my name, this I will do, that the Father may be glorified in the Son.

John 15:7 If you abide in me, and my words abide in you, ask whatever you wish, and it will be done for you.

1-John 5:14 And this is the confidence that we have toward Him, that if we ask anything according to His will He hears us.

Colossians 4:2 Continue steadfastly in **prayer**, being watchful in it with thanksgiving.

1-Samuel 1:27 For this child I **prayed**; and the Lord hath given me my petition which I asked of Him:

Luke 22:46 Rise and **pray**, lest ye enter into temptation.

2-Kings 6:17 And Elisha **prayed**, and said, Lord, I pray thee, open his eyes, that he may see. And the Lord opened the eyes of the young man; and he saw: and, behold, the mountain was full of horses and chariots of fire round about Elisha.

2-Chronicles 7:14 If my people, which are called by My name, shall humble themselves, and **pray**, and seek My face, and turn from their wicked ways; then will I hear from Heaven, and will forgive their sin, and will heal their land.

Luke 22:42-45 Father, if thou be willing, remove this cup from me: nevertheless not my will, but thine, be done. And there appeared an Angel unto Him from Heaven, strengthening Him. And being in agony He **prayed** more earnestly: and His sweat was as it were great drops of blood falling down to the ground.

Psalm 55:17 Evening and morning and at noon I will **pray**, and cry aloud, and He shall hear my voice.

Numbers 11:2 And the people cried unto Moses; and when Moses **prayed** unto the Lord, the fire was quenched.

Numbers 21:7 Therefore the people came to Moses, and said, we have sinned, for we have spoken against the Lord, and against thee; **pray** unto the Lord, that He take away the serpents from us. And Moses **prayed** for the people.

Romans 1:9 Without ceasing I make mention of you always in my **prayers**.

2-Timothy 1:3 Without ceasing I have remembrance of thee in my **prayers** night and day.

Psalm 121:1-8 I will lift up mine eyes unto the hills, from whence cometh my help. My help cometh from the L ORD, which made Heaven and earth. He will not suffer thy foot to be moved: He that keepeth thee will not slumber. Behold, He that keepeth Israel shall neither slumber nor sleep. The L ORD is thy keeper: the L ORD is thy shade upon thy right hand. The sun shall not smite thee by day, nor the moon by night. The L ORD shall preserve thee from all evil: He shall preserve thy soul. The L ORD shall preserve thy going out and thy coming in from this time forth, and even for evermore.

Luke 18:10-14 Two men went up into the temple to **pray**; the one a Pharisee, and the other a publican. The Pharisee stood and **prayed** thus with himself, God, I thank thee, that I am not as other men are, extortioners, unjust, adulterers, or even as this publican. I fast twice in the week, I give tithes of all that I possess. And the publican, standing afar off, would not lift up so much as his eyes unto Heaven, but smote upon his breast, saying, **God be merciful to me a sinner.** I tell you, this man went down to his house justified rather than the other: for every one that exalteth himself shall be abased; and he that humbleth himself shall be exalted.

Matthew 6:7-15 But when ye **pray**, use not vain repetitions, as the heathen do: for they think that they shall be heard for their much speaking. Be not ye therefore like unto them: for your Father knoweth what things ye have need of, before ye ask Him. **After this manner therefore pray ye:** Our Father which art in Heaven, Hallowed be thy name. Thy kingdom come, Thy will be done in earth, as it is in Heaven. Give us this day our daily bread. And forgive us our debts, as we forgive our debtors. And lead us not into temptation, But deliver us from evil: For thine is the kingdom, and the power, and the glory, for ever. Amen. For if ye forgive men their trespasses, your Heavenly Father will also forgive you: But if ye forgive not men their trespasses, neither will your Father forgive your trespasses.

Joshua 10:12-14 Then spake Joshua to the LORD in the day when the LORD delivered up the Amorites before the children of Israel, and he said in the sight of Israel, **Sun**, stand thou still upon Gibeon; and thou, **Moon**, in the valley of Ajalon. And the **Sun** stood still, and the **Moon** stayed, until the people had avenged themselves upon their enemies. Is not this written in the book of Jasher? So the **Sun** stood still in the midst of Heaven, and hasted not to go down about a whole day. **And there was no day like that before it or after it, that the LORD hearkened unto the voice of a man:** for the LORD fought for Israel.

1-Samuel 12:16-18 Now therefore stand and see this great thing, which the LORD will do before your eyes. Is it not wheat harvest to day? I will call unto the LORD, and he shall send **thunder and rain**; that ye may perceive and see that your wickedness is great, which ye have done in the sight of the LORD, in asking you a king. So Samuel called unto the LORD; and the LORD sent **thunder and rain** that day: and all the people greatly feared the LORD and Samuel.

1-Kings 17:1, 18:1, 41-42, 44-45 And Elijah the Tishbite, who was of the inhabitants of Gilead, said unto Ahab, As the LORD God of Israel liveth, before whom I stand, there shall not be **dew nor rain** these years, but according to my word. And it came to pass after many days, that the word of the LORD came to Elijah in the third year, saying, Go, shew thyself unto Ahab; and I will send **rain** upon the earth. And Elijah said unto Ahab, Get thee up, eat and drink; for there is a sound of abundance of **rain**. So Ahab went up to eat and to drink. And Elijah went up to the top of Carmel; and he cast himself down upon the earth, and put his face between his knees, And it came to pass at the seventh time, that he said, Behold, there ariseth a little cloud out of the sea, like a man's hand. And he said, Go up, say unto Ahab, Prepare thy chariot, and get thee down that the **rain** stop thee not. And it came to pass in the mean while, that the

Heaven was black with clouds and wind, and there was a great **rain**.

James 5:17-18 Elias was a man subject to like passions as we are, and he prayed earnestly that it might not **rain**: and it **rained** not on the earth by the space of three years and six months. And he prayed again, and the Heaven gave **rain**, and the earth brought forth her fruit.

2-Kings 6:18 And when they came down to him, Elisha prayed unto the Lord, and said, Smite this people, I pray thee, with **blindness**. And He smote them with **blindness** according to the word of Elisha.

2-Kings 20:1-6 In those days was Hezekiah sick unto death. And the prophet Isaiah the son of Amoz came to him, and said unto him, Thus saith the Lord, Set thine house in order; for thou shalt die, and not live. Then he turned his face to the wall, and **prayed unto the Lord**, saying, I beseech thee, O Lord, remember now how I have walked before thee in truth and with a perfect heart, and have done that which is good in thy sight. And Hezekiah wept sore. And it came to pass, afore Isaiah was gone out into the middle court, that the word of the Lord came to him, saying, Turn again, and tell Hezekiah the captain of my people, Thus saith the Lord, the God of David thy Father, **I have heard thy prayer**, I have seen thy tears: behold, I will heal thee: on the third day thou shalt go up unto the house of the Lord. And **I will add unto thy days fifteen years;** and I will deliver thee and this city out of the hand of the king of Assyria; and I will defend this city for mine own sake, and for my servant David's sake.

Psalm 34:1 I shall bless the Lord at all times; His **praise** shall continually be in my mouth.

Luke 19:40 I tell you that, if these should hold their peace, the stones would immediately cry out.

Psalm 150:1-6 Praise ye the LORD. Praise God in His sanctuary: praise Him in the firmament of his power. Praise Him for His mighty acts: praise Him according to His excellent greatness. Praise Him with the sound of the trumpet: praise Him with the psaltery and harp. Praise Him with the timbrel and dance: praise Him with stringed instruments and organs. Praise Him upon the loud cymbals: praise Him upon the high sounding cymbals. **Let every thing that hath breath praise the LORD.** Praise ye the LORD.

Psalm 111:1, 3 **Praise** ye the LORD. I will praise the LORD with my whole heart, in the assembly of the upright, and in the congregation. From the rising of the sun unto the going down of the same, the Lord's name is to be **praised**.

Psalm 112:1 **Praise** ye the LORD. Blessed is the man that feareth the LORD, that delighteth greatly in His commandments.

Psalm 113:1 **Praise** ye the LORD. Praise, O ye servants of the LORD, praise the name of the LORD.

Psalm 117:1 O **praise** the LORD, all ye nations: praise Him, all ye people.

Psalm 135:1 **Praise** ye the LORD. Praise ye the name of the LORD; praise Him, O ye servants of the LORD.

Psalm 91:11-12 For He shall give his angels charge over thee, to keep thee in all thy ways. They shall bear thee up in their hands, lest thou dash thy foot against a stone.

Proverbs 27:2 **Let another man praise thee, and not thine own mouth;** a stranger, and not thine own lips.

Job 1:21-22 Naked came I out of my mother's womb, and naked shall I return thither: the Lord gave, and the Lord hath taken away; **blessed** be the name of the Lord. In all this, Job sinned not, nor charged God foolishly.

Numbers 6:22-26 And the LORD spake unto Moses, saying, Speak unto Aaron and unto his sons, saying, On this wise ye shall bless the children of Israel, saying unto them, **The LORD bless thee, and keep thee: The LORD make His face shine upon thee, and be gracious unto thee: The LORD lift up His countenance upon thee, and give thee peace.**

Psalm 103:1-10, 15-22 **Bless the LORD, O my soul**: and all that is within me, bless His holy name. **Bless the LORD,** O my soul, and forget not all His benefits: Who forgiveth all thine iniquities; Who healeth all thy diseases; Who redeemeth thy life from destruction; Who crowneth thee with lovingkindness and tender mercies; Who satisfieth thy mouth with good things; so that thy youth is renewed like the eagle's. The LORD executeth righteousness and judgment for all that are oppressed. He made known His ways unto Moses, His acts unto the children of Israel. **The LORD is merciful and gracious, slow to anger, and plenteous in mercy.** He will not always chide: neither will He keep His anger for ever. He hath not dealt with us after our sins; nor rewarded us according to our iniquities. As for man, his days are as grass: as a flower of the field, so he flourisheth. For the wind passeth over it, and it is gone; and the place thereof shall know it no more. **But the mercy of the LORD is from everlasting to everlasting upon them that fear Him, and His righteousness unto children's children; To such as keep his covenant, and to those that remember His commandments to do them.** The LORD hath prepared His throne in the Heavens; and His kingdom ruleth over all. **Bless the LORD,** ye his angels, that excel in strength, that do His commandments, hearkening unto the voice of His word. **Bless ye the LORD,** all ye His hosts; ye ministers of His, that do His pleasure. **Bless the LORD,** all

39

His works in all places of His dominion: **bless the LORD, O my soul.**

1-Thessalonians 5:16 Rejoice evermore.

Psalm 106:1 **Praise** ye the LORD. O give thanks unto the LORD; for He is good: for His mercy endureth for ever.

Psalm 136:1-26 (for His mercy endureth for ever) O give thanks unto the LORD; for He is good: for His mercy endureth for ever. O give thanks unto the God of gods: for His mercy endureth for ever. O give thanks to the Lord of Lords: for His mercy endureth for ever. To Him who alone doeth great wonders: for His mercy endureth for ever. To Him that by wisdom made the Heavens: for His mercy endureth for ever. To Him that stretched out the earth above the waters: for His mercy endureth for ever. To Him that made great lights: for His mercy endureth for ever: The sun to rule by day: for His mercy endureth for ever: The moon and stars to rule by night: for His mercy endureth for ever. To Him that smote Egypt in their firstborn: for His mercy endureth for ever: And brought out Israel from among them: for His mercy endureth for ever: With a strong hand, and with a stretched out arm: for His mercy endureth for ever. To Him which divided the Red sea into parts: for His mercy endureth for ever: And made Israel to pass through the midst of it: for His mercy endureth for ever: But overthrew Pharaoh and his host in the Red sea: for His mercy endureth for ever. To Him which led His people through the wilderness: for His mercy endureth for ever. To Him which smote great kings: for His mercy endureth for ever: And slew famous kings: for His mercy endureth for ever: Sihon king of the Amorites: for His mercy endureth for ever: And Og the king of Bashan: for His mercy endureth for ever: And gave their land for an heritage: for His mercy endureth for ever: Even an heritage unto Israel his servant: for His mercy endureth for ever. Who remembered us in our low estate: for His mercy endureth for ever: And hath redeemed us from our enemies: for His mercy endureth for ever. Who giveth food to all flesh: for His mercy endureth for ever. O give thanks unto the God of Heaven: for His mercy endureth for ever.

Ecclesiastes 12:13 Let us hear the conclusion of the whole matter: **Fear** God, and keep His commandments: for this is the whole duty of man.

Psalm 111:10 The **fear** of the LORD is the beginning of wisdom: a good understanding have all they that do His commandments: His praise endureth for ever.

Proverbs 1:7 The **fear** of the Lord is the beginning of knowledge, but fools despise wisdom and instruction.

Proverbs 3:7 Be not wise in thine own eyes: **fear** the Lord, and depart from evil.

Psalm 103:11-14 For as the Heaven is high above the earth, so great is His mercy toward us that **fear** Him. As far as the east is from the west, so far hath He removed our transgressions from us. Like as a Father pitieth his children, so the Lord pitieth us that **fear** Him. For He knoweth our frame; **He remembereth that we are dust.**

Psalm 33:8 Let all the earth **fear** the Lord: let all the inhabitants of the world stand in awe of Him.

Psalm 128:4 Behold, that thus shall the man be blessed that **feareth** the Lord.

Ecclesiastes 5:4-5 Better is it that thou shouldest not **vow** unto God, than that thou shouldest **vow** and not pay. God has no pleasure in fools.

Deuteronomy 23:21-23 When thou shalt **vow** a **vow** unto the Lord thy God, thou shalt not slack to pay it: for the Lord thy God will surely require it of thee; and it would be sin in thee.

Matthew 22:37-38 Thou shalt **love** the Lord thy God with all thy heart, and with all thy soul, and with all thy mind. This is the first and great commandment.

Mark 12:31 And the second is Thou shalt love thy neighbor as thyself. **There is none other commandment greater than these.**

Romans 8:28-39 And we know that all things work together for good to them that love God, to them who are the called according to His purpose. For whom He did foreknow, He also did predestinate to be conformed to the image of His Son, that He might be the firstborn among many brethren. Moreover whom He did predestinate, them He also called: and whom He called, them He also justified: and whom He justified, them He also glorified. What shall we then say to these things? **If God be for us, who can be against us? He that spared not his own Son,** but delivered Him up for us all, how shall He not with Him also freely give us all things? Who shall lay any thing to the charge of God's elect? It is God that justifieth. Who is he that condemneth? It is Christ that died, yea rather, that is risen again, who is even at the right hand of God, who also maketh intercession for us. **Who shall separate us from the love of Christ?** shall tribulation, or distress, or persecution, or famine, or nakedness, or peril, or sword? As it is written, **For thy sake we are killed all the day long; we are accounted as sheep for the slaughter.** Nay, in all these things we are more than conquerors through Him that loved us. **For I am persuaded, that neither death, nor life, nor angels, nor principalities, nor powers, nor things present, nor things to come, Nor height, nor depth, nor any other creature, shall be able to separate us from the love of God, which is in Christ Jesus our Lord.**

Ephesians 2:8-10 For by grace are ye saved through faith; and that not of yourselves: it is the **gift of God**: Not of works, lest any man should boast.   For we are His workmanship, created in Christ Jesus unto good works, which God hath before ordained that we should walk in them.

Romans 6:23 For the wages of sin is death, but the **gift of God** is eternal life in Christ Jesus our Lord.

Acts 2:38   Then Peter said unto them, Repent, and be baptized every one of you in the name of Jesus Christ for the remission of sins, and ye shall receive the **gift of the Holy Ghost**.

Psalm 46:10 Be still, and know that I am God: I will be **exalted** among the heathen, I will be **exalted** in the earth.

Psalm 34:3 O magnify the Lord with me, and let us **exalt** His name together.

Psalm 57:5, 11 Be thou **exalted**, O God, above the Heavens; let thy glory be above all the earth. Be thou **exalted**, O God, above the Heavens: let thy glory be above all the earth.

Psalm 97:9 For thou, Lord, art high above all the earth: thou art **exalted** far above all Gods.

Psalm 99:5, 9 **Exalt** ye the Lord our God, and worship at His footstool; for He is holy. **Exalt** the Lord our God, and worship at His holy hill; for the Lord our God is holy.

Psalm 108:5 Be thou **exalted**, O God, above the Heavens: and thy glory above all the earth.

Isaiah 25:1 O Lord, thou art my God; I will **exalt** thee, I will praise thy name; for thou hast done wonderful things; thy counsels of old are faithfulness and truth.

Proverbs 3:5-6 **Trust** in the Lord with all thine heart; and lean not unto thine own understanding. In all thy ways acknowledge Him, and He shall direct thy paths.

Psalm 118:8-9 It is better to **trust** in the LORD than to put confidence in man. It is better to **trust** in the LORD than to put confidence in princes.

Joshua 24:15 And if it seem evil unto you to serve the Lord, choose you this day whom ye will serve; but as for me and my house, we will **serve the Lord.**

Isaiah 40:31 But they that **wait** upon the Lord shall renew their strength; they shall mount up with wings as eagles; they shall run, and not be weary; and they shall walk, and not faint.

Psalm 27:14 **Wait** on the Lord: be of good courage, and He shall strengthen thine heart: **wait,** I say, on the Lord.

Deuteronomy 5:6-21   I am the L ORD thy God, which brought thee out of the land of Egypt, from the house of bondage.   Thou shalt have none other gods before Me. Thou shalt not make thee any graven image, or any likeness of any thing that is in Heaven above, or that is in the earth beneath, or that is in the waters beneath the earth: Thou shalt not bow down thyself unto them, nor serve them: **for I the L ORD thy God am a jealous God, visiting the iniquity of the fathers upon the children unto the third and fourth generation of them that hate Me, And shewing mercy unto thousands of them that love Me and keep My commandments.**   Thou shalt not take the name of the L ORD thy God in vain: for the L ORD will not hold him guiltless that taketh His name in vain.   Keep the Sabbath day to sanctify it, as the L ORD thy God hath commanded thee.   Six days thou shalt labour, and do all thy work: But the seventh day is the Sabbath of the L ORD thy God: in it thou shalt not do any work, thou, nor thy son, nor thy daughter, nor thy manservant, nor thy maidservant, nor thine ox, nor thine ass, nor any of thy cattle, nor thy stranger that is within thy gates; that thy manservant and thy maidservant may rest as well as thou.   And remember that thou wast a servant in the land of Egypt, and that the L ORD thy God brought thee out thence through a mighty hand and by a stretched out arm: therefore the L ORD thy God commanded thee to keep the Sabbath day.   Honour thy father and thy mother, as the L ORD thy God hath commanded thee; that thy days may be prolonged, and that it may go well with thee, in the land which the L ORD thy God giveth thee.   Thou shalt not kill.   Neither shalt thou commit adultery.   Neither shalt thou steal.   Neither shalt thou bear false witness against thy neighbour.   Neither shalt thou desire thy neighbour's wife, neither shalt thou covet thy neighbour's house, his field, or his manservant, or his maidservant, his ox, or his ass, or any thing that is thy neighbour's.

John 13:34-35 **A new commandment I give unto you,** That ye love one another; as I have loved you, **that ye also love one another.** By this shall all men know that ye are My disciples, if ye have love one to another.

John 14:15, 23 If ye love Me, keep my **commandments.** If a man **love** Me, he will keep My words.

Galatians 5:14 For all the law is fulfilled in one word, even in this; thou shalt love thy neighbor as thyself.

Matthew 19:16-30 And, behold, one came and said unto Him, Good Master, what good thing shall I do, that I may have eternal life? And He said unto him, Why callest thou Me good? **there is none good but one, that is, God: but if thou wilt enter into life, keep the commandments.** He saith unto him, Which? Jesus said, Thou shalt do no murder, Thou shalt not commit adultery, Thou shalt not steal, Thou shalt not bear false witness, Honour thy father and thy mother: and, Thou shalt love thy neighbour as thyself. The young man saith unto him, **All these things have I kept from my youth up: what lack I yet? Jesus said unto him, If thou wilt be perfect, go and sell that thou hast, and give to the poor, and thou shalt have treasure in Heaven: and come and follow Me.** But when the young man heard that saying, he went away sorrowful: for he had great possessions. Then said Jesus unto his disciples, Verily I say unto you, That a rich man shall hardly enter into the kingdom of Heaven. **And again I say unto you, It is easier for a camel to go through the eye of a needle, than for a rich man to enter into the kingdom of God.** When His disciples heard it, they were exceedingly amazed, saying, Who then can be saved? But Jesus beheld them, and said unto them, **With men this is impossible; but with God all things are possible.** Then answered Peter and said unto him, Behold, **we have forsaken all, and followed thee; what shall we have therefore?** And Jesus said unto them, Verily I say unto you, That **ye which have followed Me, in the regeneration when the Son of man shall sit in the throne of His glory, ye also shall sit upon twelve thrones, judging the twelve tribes of Israel. And every one that hath forsaken houses, or brethren, or sisters, or**

father, or mother, or wife, or children, or lands, for My name's sake, shall receive an hundredfold, and shall inherit everlasting life. But many that are first shall be last; and the last shall be first.

John 15:9-17 As the Father hath loved Me, so have I loved you: continue ye in my love. If ye keep My **commandments,** ye shall abide in My love; even as I have kept My Father's **commandments,** and abide in His love. These things have I spoken unto you, that My joy might remain in you, and that your joy might be full. This is My **commandment,** That ye love one another, as I have loved you. Greater love hath no man than this, that a man lay down his life for his friends. Ye are my friends, if ye do whatsoever I **command** you. Henceforth I call you not servants; for the servant knoweth not what his Lord doeth: but I have called you friends; for all things that I have heard of My Father I have made known unto you. Ye have not chosen Me, but I have chosen you, and ordained you, that ye should go and bring forth fruit, and that your fruit should remain: that whatsoever ye shall ask of the Father in My name, he may give it you. These things I **command** you, that ye love one another.

Psalm 30:5 For His anger is but for a moment, His **favor** is for life; **Weeping may endure for a night, But joy comes in the morning.**

Proverbs 12:2 A good man obtains **favor** from the Lord, But a man of wicked intentions He will condemn.

Proverbs 8:35 For whoever finds Me finds life, And obtains **favor** from the Lord;

Proverbs 3:4 And so find **favor** and high esteem in the sight of God and man.

Proverbs 18:22 Whosoever findeth a wife findeth a good thing, and obtaineth **favour** of God.

Proverbs 11:27 He who earnestly seeks good finds **favor**, But trouble will come to him who seeks evil.

Proverbs 14:9 Fools make a mock at sin: but among the righteous there is **favour**.

Proverbs 28:23 He who rebukes a man will find more **favor** afterward than he who flatters with the tongue.

Luke 1:30 Then the angel said to her, "Do not be afraid, Mary, for you have found **favor** with God."

Luke 2:52 And Jesus increased in wisdom and stature, and in **favor** with God and men.

1-Corinthians 2:9 **Eyes have not seen,** ears haven't heard, and neither has it entered into the hearts of those, the things which God hath prepared for them who love Him.

Psalm 84:11 The Lord will give grace and glory: **no good thing will He withhold from them that walk uprightly.**

Psalm 24:1 The earth is the Lord's, and the fulness thereof; the world, and they that dwell therein.

Psalm 100:3 Know ye that the Lord He is God: it is He that hath made us, and not we ourselves; we are His people, and the sheep of His pasture.

Psalm 103:12 As far as the east is from the west, so far hath He removed our transgressions from us.

Isaiah 55:8-11 **For My thoughts are not your thoughts, neither are your ways My ways, saith the LORD. For as the Heavens are higher than the earth, so are My ways higher than your ways, and My thoughts than your thoughts.** For as the rain cometh down, and the snow from Heaven, and returneth not thither, but watereth the earth, and maketh it bring forth and bud, that it may give seed to the sower, and bread to the eater: So shall My word be that goeth forth out of My mouth: it shall not return unto Me void, but it shall accomplish that which I please, and it shall prosper in the thing whereto I sent it.

Jeremiah 32:26-28 Then came the word of the LORD unto Jeremiah, saying, Behold, I am the LORD, the God of all flesh: is there anything too hard for Me?

Colossians 1:16-17 For by Him were all things created, that are in Heaven, and that are in earth, visible and invisible, whether they be thrones, or dominions, or principalities, or powers: all things were created by Him, and for Him: And He is before all things, and by Him all things consist.

Job 38:4 Where were you when I laid the foundations of the earth? Tell Me, if you have understanding.

Romans 3:23 For all have sinned and fall short of the glory of God;

Hebrews 11: 1-13, 17-35 **Now faith is the substance of things hoped for, the evidence of things not seen.** For by it the elders obtained a good report. Through **faith** we understand that the worlds were framed by the word of God, so that things which are seen were not made of things which do appear. By **faith** Abel offered unto God a more excellent sacrifice than Cain, by which he obtained witness that he was righteous, God testifying of his gifts: and by it he being dead yet speaketh. By **faith** Enoch was translated that he should not see death; and was not found, because God had translated him: for before his translation he had this testimony, that he pleased God. **But without faith it is impossible to please Him: for he that cometh to God must believe that He is, and that He is a rewarder of them that diligently seek Him.** By **faith** Noah, being warned of God of things not seen as yet, moved with fear, prepared an ark to the saving of his house; by the which he condemned the world, and became heir of the righteousness which is by faith. By **faith** Abraham, when he was called to go out into a place which he should after receive for an inheritance, obeyed; and he went out, not knowing whither he went. By **faith** he sojourned in the land of promise, as in a strange country, dwelling in tabernacles with Isaac and Jacob, the heirs with him of the same promise: For he looked for a city which hath foundations, whose builder and maker is God. Through **faith** also Sara herself received strength to conceive seed, and was delivered of a child when she was past age, because she judged him faithful who had promised. Therefore sprang there even of one, and him as good as dead, so many as the stars of the sky in multitude, and as the sand which is by the sea shore innumerable. These all died in **faith**, not having received the promises, but having seen them afar off, and were persuaded of them, and embraced them, and confessed that they were strangers and pilgrims on the earth. By **faith** Abraham, when he was tried, offered up Isaac: and he that had received the promises offered up his only begotten son, Of whom it was said, That in Isaac shall thy seed be called:

51

Accounting that God was able to raise him up, even from the dead; from whence also he received him in a figure. By **faith** Isaac blessed Jacob and Esau concerning things to come. By **faith** Jacob, when he was a dying, blessed both the sons of Joseph; and worshipped, leaning upon the top of his staff. By **faith** Joseph, when he died, made mention of the departing of the children of Israel; and gave commandment concerning his bones. By **faith** Moses, when he was born, was hid three months of his parents, because they saw he was a proper child; and they were not afraid of the king's commandment. By **faith** Moses, when he was come to years, refused to be called the son of Pharaoh's daughter; Choosing rather to suffer affliction with the people of God, than to enjoy the pleasures of sin for a season; esteeming the reproach of Christ greater riches than the treasures in Egypt: for he had respect unto the recompence of the reward. By **faith** he forsook Egypt, not fearing the wrath of the king: for he endured, as seeing him who is invisible. Through **faith** he kept the passover, and the sprinkling of blood, lest He that destroyed the firstborn should touch them. By **faith** they passed through the Red sea as by dry land: which the Egyptians assaying to do were drowned. By **faith** the walls of Jericho fell down, after they were compassed about seven days. By **faith** the harlot Rahab perished not with them that believed not, when she had received the spies with peace. And what shall I more say? for the time would fail me to tell of Gedeon, and of Barak, and of Samson, and of Jephthae; of David also, and Samuel, and of the prophets: Who through **faith** subdued kingdoms, wrought righteousness, obtained promises, stopped the mouths of lions. Quenched the violence of fire, escaped the edge of the sword, out of weakness were made strong, waxed valiant in fight, turned to flight the armies of the aliens. Women received their dead raised to life again:

Mark 11:20-24 And in the morning, as they passed by, they saw the fig tree dried up from the roots. And Peter calling to remembrance saith unto him, Master, behold, the fig tree which thou cursedst is withered away. And Jesus answering saith unto them, Have **faith** in God. For verily I say unto you, That whosoever shall say unto this mountain, Be thou removed, and be thou cast into the sea; and shall not doubt in his heart, but shall believe that those things which he saith shall come to pass; he shall have whatsoever he saith. Therefore I say unto you, What things soever ye desire, when ye pray, believe that ye receive them, and ye shall have them.

James 2:17 Even so **faith**, if it hath not works, is dead, being alone.

Mark 16:18 **They shall lay hands on the sick,** and they shall recover.

Luke 17:5-6 And the apostles said unto the Lord, Increase our **faith**. And the Lord said, If ye had **faith** as a grain of mustard seed, ye might say unto this sycamine tree, Be thou plucked up by the root, and be thou planted in the sea; and it should obey you.

James 5:14-16 **Is any sick among you?** let him call for the elders of the church; and let them pray over him, anointing him with oil in the name of the Lord: And the prayer of faith shall save the sick, and the Lord shall raise him up; and if he have committed sins, they shall be forgiven him. Confess your faults one to another, and pray one for another, that ye may be healed. **The effectual fervent prayer of a righteous man availeth much.**

Isaiah 53:5 But He was wounded for our transgressions, He was bruised for our iniquities: the chastisement of our peace was upon Him; and **with His stripes we are healed.**

Philippians 4:7, 13 And the peace of God, which passeth all understanding, shall keep your hearts and minds through Christ Jesus. I can do all things through Christ who strengthens me.

2-Kings 4:8-26, 35 And it fell on a day, that Elisha passed to Shunem, where was a great woman; and she constrained him to eat bread. And so it was, that as oft as he passed by, he turned in thither to eat bread. And she said unto her husband, Behold now, I perceive that this is an holy man of God, which passeth by us continually. Let us make a little

53

chamber, I pray thee, on the wall; and let us set for him there a bed, and a table, and a stool, and a candlestick: and it shall be, when he cometh to us, that he shall turn in thither. And it fell on a day, that he came thither, and he turned into the chamber, and lay there. And he said to Gehazi his servant, Call this Shunammite. And when he had called her, she stood before him. And he said unto him, Say now unto her, Behold, thou hast been careful for us with all this care; what is to be done for thee? wouldest thou be spoken for to the king, or to the captain of the host? And she answered, I dwell among mine own people. And he said, What then is to be done for her? And Gehazi answered, Verily she hath no child, and her husband is old. And he said, Call her. And when he had called her, she stood in the door. And he said, About this season, according to the time of life, thou shalt embrace a son. And she said, Nay, my Lord, thou man of God, do not lie unto thine handmaid. And the woman conceived, and bare a son at that season that Elisha had said unto her, according to the time of life. And when the child was grown, it fell on a day, that he went out to his father to the reapers. And he said unto his father, My head, my head. And he said to a lad, Carry him to his mother. And when he had taken him, and brought him to his mother, he sat on her knees till noon, and then died. And she went up, and laid him on the bed of the man of God, and shut the door upon him, and went out. And she called unto her husband, and said, Send me, I pray thee, one of the young men, and one of the asses, that I may run to the man of God, and come again. And he said, Wherefore wilt thou go to him to day? it is neither new moon, nor Sabbath. And she said, **It shall be well.** Then she saddled an ass, and said to her servant, Drive, and go forward; slack not thy riding for me, except I bid thee. So she went and came unto the man of God to mount Carmel. And it came to pass, when the man of God saw her afar off, that he said to Gehazi his servant, Behold, yonder is that Shunammite: Run now, I pray thee, to meet her, and say unto her, Is it well with thee? is it well with thy husband? is it well with the child? And she answered, **It is well**: Then he returned, and walked in the house to and fro; and went up, and stretched himself upon him: and the child sneezed seven times, and the child opened his eyes.

Matthew 5:45 His sun will rise on the **evil** and the **good**. His rain will fall on the **just** and the **unjust**.

Proverbs 16:4 The Lord hath made all things for Himself, yea, even the wicked for the day of **evil**.

Psalm 34:14-20 Depart from evil, and do good; seek peace, and pursue it. The eyes of the LORD are upon the **righteous**, and His ears are open unto their cry. The face of the LORD is against them that do evil, to cut off the remembrance of them from the earth. The righteous cry, and the LORD heareth, and delivereth them out of all their troubles. The LORD is nigh unto them that are of a broken heart; and saveth such as be of a contrite spirit. Many are the afflictions of the **righteous**: but the LORD delivereth him out of them all. He keepeth all his bones: not one of them is broken.

1-Peter 3:12 For the eyes of the Lord are over the **righteous**, and His ears are open unto their prayers: but the face of the Lord is against them that do evil.

Job 34:19 Yet He is not partial to princes, nor does He regard the rich more than the poor; for they are all the work of His hands.

James 2:9 But if ye have **respect to persons**, ye commit sin.

Romans 2:11 For there is no **respect of persons** with God.

Ephesians 6:9 Your Master also is in Heaven; neither is there **respect of persons** with Him.

Acts 10:34 Of a truth I perceive that God is no **respecter of persons**.

1-Peter 1:17 The Father, who without **respect of persons** judgeth according to every man's work.

Colossians 3:25 But he that doeth wrong shall receive for the wrong which he hath done: and there is no **respect of persons**.

Ecclesiastes 3:1 To every thing there is a season, and a time to every purpose under the Heaven.

Judges 7:2-7 And the LORD said to Gideon, The people who are with you are too many for Me to give the Midianites into their hands. Proclaim in the hearing of the people, saying, whoever is fearful and afraid, let him turn and depart at once from Mount Gilead. And twenty-two thousand of the people returned, and ten thousand remained. But the LORD said to Gideon, The people are still too many; bring them down to the water, and I will test them for you there. And the LORD said to Gideon, everyone who laps from the water with his tongue, as a dog laps, you shall set apart by himself; likewise everyone who gets down on his knees to drink. And the number of those who **lapped, putting their hand to their mouth,** was three hundred men; but all the rest of the people got down on their knees to drink water. Then the LORD said to Gideon, **By the three hundred men who lapped** I will save you, and deliver the Midianites into your hand. Let all the other people go, every man to his place.

Deuteronomy 20:10-18 When thou comest nigh unto a city to fight against it, then proclaim peace unto it. And it shall be, if it make thee answer of peace, and open unto thee, then it shall be, that all the people that is found therein shall be tributaries unto thee, and they shall serve thee. And if it will make no peace with thee, but will make war against thee, then thou shalt besiege it: And when the LORD thy God hath delivered it into thine hands, thou shalt smite every male thereof with the edge of the sword: But the women, and the little ones, and the cattle, and all that is in the city, even all the spoil thereof, shalt thou take unto thyself; and thou shalt eat the spoil of thine enemies, which the LORD thy God hath given thee. Thus shalt thou do unto all the cities which are very far off from thee, which are not of the cities of these nations. **But of the cities of these people, which the LORD thy God doth give thee for an**

inheritance, thou shalt save alive nothing that breatheth: **But thou shalt utterly destroy them;** namely, the Hittites, and the Amorites, the Canaanites, and the Perizzites, the Hivites, and the Jebusites; as the LORD thy God hath commanded thee: **That they teach you not to do after all their abominations, which they have done unto their gods;** so should ye sin against the LORD your God.

Exodus 17:8-16 Then came Amalek, and fought with Israel in Rephidim. And Moses said unto Joshua, Choose us out men, and go out, fight with Amalek: to morrow I will stand on the top of the hill with the rod of God in mine hand. So Joshua did as Moses had said to him, and fought with Amalek: and Moses, Aaron, and Hur went up to the top of the hill. And it came to pass, when Moses held up his hand, that Israel prevailed: and when he let down his hand, Amalek prevailed. But Moses hands were heavy; and they took a stone, and put it under him, and he sat thereon; and Aaron and Hur stayed up his hands, the one on the one side, and the other on the other side; and his hands were steady until the going down of the sun. And Joshua discomfited Amalek and his people with the edge of the sword. **And the LORD said unto Moses,** Write this for a memorial in a book, and rehearse it in the ears of Joshua: **for I will utterly put out the remembrance of Amalek from under heaven.** And Moses built an altar, and called the name of it Jehovahnissi: For he said, **Because the LORD hath sworn that the LORD will have war with Amalek from generation to generation.**

1-Samuel 15:1-35 Samuel also said unto Saul, The LORD sent me to anoint thee to be king over his people, over Israel: now therefore hearken thou unto the voice of the words of the LORD. Thus saith the LORD of hosts, I remember that which Amalek did to Israel, how he laid wait for him in the way, when he came up from Egypt. Now go and smite Amalek, and utterly destroy all that they have, and spare them not; but slay both man and woman, infant and suckling, ox and sheep, camel and ass. And Saul gathered the people together, and numbered them in Telaim, two hundred thousand footmen, and ten thousand men of Judah. And Saul came to a city of

Amalek, and laid wait in the valley. And Saul said unto the Kenites, Go, depart, get you down from among the Amalekites, lest I destroy you with them: for ye shewed kindness to all the children of Israel, when they came up out of Egypt. So the Kenites departed from among the Amalekites. And Saul smote the Amalekites from Havilah until thou comest to Shur, that is over against Egypt. And he took Agag the king of the Amalekites alive, and **utterly destroyed** all the people with the edge of the sword. But Saul and the people spared Agag, and the best of the sheep, and of the oxen, and of the fatlings, and the lambs, and all that was good, and would not **utterly destroy** them: but every thing that was vile and refuse, that they **destroyed utterly**. Then came the word of the LORD unto Samuel, saying, It repenteth me that I have set up Saul to be king: for he is turned back from following me, and hath not performed my commandments. And it grieved Samuel; and he cried unto the LORD all night. And when Samuel rose early to meet Saul in the morning, it was told Samuel, saying, Saul came to Carmel, and, behold, he set him up a place, and is gone about, and passed on, and gone down to Gilgal. And Samuel came to Saul: and Saul said unto him, Blessed be thou of the LORD: I have performed the commandment of the LORD. And Samuel said, What meaneth then this bleating of the sheep in mine ears, and the lowing of the oxen which I hear? And Saul said, They have brought them from the Amalekites: for the people spared the best of the sheep and of the oxen, to sacrifice unto the LORD thy God; and the rest we have **utterly destroyed**. Then Samuel said unto Saul, Stay, and I will tell thee what the LORD hath said to me this night. And he said unto him, Say on. And Samuel said, When thou wast little in thine own sight, wast thou not made the head of the tribes of Israel, and the LORD anointed thee king over Israel? And the LORD sent thee on a journey, and said, Go and **utterly destroy** the sinners the Amalekites, and fight against them until they be consumed. Wherefore then didst thou not obey the voice of the LORD, but didst fly upon the spoil, and didst evil in the sight of the LORD? And Saul said unto Samuel, Yea, I have obeyed the voice of the LORD, and have gone the way which the LORD sent me, and have brought Agag the king of Amalek, and have **utterly**

59

destroyed the Amalekites. But the people took of the spoil, sheep and oxen, the chief of the things which should have been **utterly destroyed**, to sacrifice unto the LORD thy God in Gilgal. And Samuel said, **Hath the LORD as great delight in burnt offerings and sacrifices, as in obeying the voice of the LORD? Behold, to obey is better than sacrifice, and to hearken than the fat of rams. For rebellion is as the sin of witchcraft, and stubbornness is as iniquity and idolatry.** Because thou hast rejected the word of the LORD, he hath also rejected thee from being king. And Saul said unto Samuel, I have sinned: for I have transgressed the commandment of the LORD, and thy words: because I feared the people, and obeyed their voice. Now therefore, I pray thee, pardon my sin, and turn again with me, that I may worship the LORD. And Samuel said unto Saul, I will not return with thee: for thou hast rejected the word of the LORD, and the LORD hath rejected thee from being king over Israel. And as Samuel turned about to go away, he laid hold upon the skirt of his mantle, and it rent. And Samuel said unto him, The LORD hath rent the kingdom of Israel from thee this day, and hath given it to a neighbour of thine, that is better than thou. And also the Strength of Israel will not lie nor repent: for he is not a man, that he should repent. Then he said, I have sinned: yet honour me now, I pray thee, before the elders of my people, and before Israel, and turn again with me, that I may worship the LORD thy God. So Samuel turned again after Saul; and Saul worshipped the LORD. Then said Samuel, Bring ye hither to me Agag the king of the Amalekites. And Agag came unto him delicately. And Agag said, Surely the bitterness of death is past. And Samuel said, As thy sword hath made women childless, so shall thy mother be childless among women. And Samuel hewed Agag in pieces before the LORD in Gilgal. Then Samuel went to Ramah; and Saul went up to his house to Gibeah of Saul. And Samuel came no more to see Saul until the day of his death: nevertheless Samuel mourned for Saul: and the LORD repented that he had made Saul king over Israel.

<u>Joshua 6:1-27</u> Now Jericho was straitly shut up because of the children of Israel: none went out, and none came in. **And the LORD said unto Joshua,** See, I have given into

thine hand Jericho, and the king thereof, and the mighty men of valour. And ye shall compass the city, all ye men of war, and go round about the city once. Thus shalt thou do six days. And seven priests shall bear before the ark seven trumpets of rams' horns: and the seventh day ye shall compass the city seven times, and the priests shall blow with the trumpets. And it shall come to pass, that when they make a long blast with the ram's horn, and when ye hear the sound of the trumpet, all the people shall shout with a great shout; and the wall of the city shall fall down flat, and the people shall ascend up every man straight before him. And Joshua the son of Nun called the priests, and said unto them, Take up the ark of the covenant, and let seven priests bear seven trumpets of rams' horns before the ark of the LORD. And he said unto the people, Pass on, and compass the city, and let him that is armed pass on before the ark of the LORD. And it came to pass, when Joshua had spoken unto the people, that the seven priests bearing the seven trumpets of rams' horns passed on before the LORD, and blew with the trumpets: and the ark of the covenant of the LORD followed them. And the armed men went before the priests that blew with the trumpets, and the rereward came after the ark, the priests going on, and blowing with the trumpets. And Joshua had commanded the people, saying, Ye shall not shout, nor make any noise with your voice, neither shall any word proceed out of your mouth, until the day I bid you shout; then shall ye shout. So the ark of the LORD compassed the city, going about it once: and they came into the camp, and lodged in the camp. And Joshua rose early in the morning, and the priests took up the ark of the LORD. And seven priests bearing seven trumpets of rams' horns before the ark of the LORD went on continually, and blew with the trumpets: and the armed men went before them; but the rereward came after the ark of the LORD, the priests going on, and blowing with the trumpets. And the second day they compassed the city once, and returned into the camp: so they did six days. And it came to pass on the seventh day, that they rose early about the dawning of the day, and compassed the city after the same manner seven times: only on that day they compassed the city seven times. And it came to pass at the seventh time, when the priests blew with the trumpets, Joshua said unto the people, Shout;

for the LORD hath given you the city. And the city shall be accursed, even it, and all that are therein, to the LORD: only Rahab the harlot shall live, she and all that are with her in the house, because she hid the messengers that we sent. And ye, in any wise keep yourselves from the accursed thing, lest ye make yourselves accursed, when ye take of the accursed thing, and make the camp of Israel a curse, and trouble it. But all the silver, and gold, and vessels of brass and iron, are consecrated unto the LORD: they shall come into the treasury of the LORD. So the people shouted when the priests blew with the trumpets: and it came to pass, when the people heard the sound of the trumpet, and the people shouted with a great shout, that the wall fell down flat, so that the people went up into the city, every man straight before him, and they took the city. And they **utterly destroyed** all that was in the city, both man and woman, young and old, and ox, and sheep, and ass, with the edge of the sword. But Joshua had said unto the two men that had spied out the country, Go into the harlot's house, and bring out thence the woman, and all that she hath, as ye sware unto her. And the young men that were spies went in, and brought out Rahab, and her father, and her mother, and her brethren, and all that she had; and they brought out all her kindred, and left them without the camp of Israel. And they burnt the city with fire, and all that was therein: only the silver, and the gold, and the vessels of brass and of iron, they put into the treasury of the house of the LORD. And Joshua saved Rahab the harlot alive, and her father's household, and all that she had; and she dwelleth in Israel even unto this day; because she hid the messengers, which Joshua sent to spy out Jericho. And Joshua adjured them at that time, saying, Cursed be the man before the LORD, that riseth up and buildeth this city Jericho: he shall lay the foundation thereof in his firstborn, and in his youngest son shall he set up the gates of it. **So the LORD was with Joshua;** and his fame was noised throughout all the country.

Joshua 7:1-26 But the children of Israel committed a trespass in the accursed thing: for Achan, the son of Carmi, the son of Zabdi, the son of Zerah, of the tribe of Judah, took of the accursed thing: **and the anger of the**

LORD was kindled against the children of Israel. And Joshua sent men from Jericho to Ai, which is beside Bethaven, on the east of Bethel, and spake unto them, saying, Go up and view the country. And the men went up and viewed Ai. And they returned to Joshua, and said unto him, Let not all the people go up; but let about two or three thousand men go up and smite Ai; and make not all the people to labour thither; for they are but few. So there went up thither of the people **about three thousand men: and they fled before the men of Ai. And the men of Ai smote of them about thirty and six men:** for they chased them from before the gate even unto Shebarim, and smote them in the going down: wherefore the hearts of the people melted, and became as water. And Joshua rent his clothes, and fell to the earth upon his face before the ark of the LORD until the eventide, he and the elders of Israel, and put dust upon their heads. And Joshua said, Alas, O LORD God, wherefore hast thou at all brought this people over Jordan, to deliver us into the hand of the Amorites, to destroy us? would to God we had been content, and dwelt on the other side Jordan! O LORD, what shall I say, when Israel turneth their backs before their enemies! For the Canaanites and all the inhabitants of the land shall hear of it, and shall environ us round, and cut off our name from the earth: and what wilt thou do unto thy great name? **And the LORD said unto Joshua,** Get thee up; wherefore liest thou thus upon thy face? Israel hath sinned, and they have also transgressed my covenant which I commanded them: for they have even taken of the accursed thing, and have also stolen, and dissembled also, and they have put it even among their own stuff. Therefore the children of Israel could not stand before their enemies, but turned their backs before their enemies, because they were accursed: **neither will I be with you any more, except ye destroy the accursed from among you.** Up, sanctify the people, and say, Sanctify yourselves against to morrow: **for thus saith the LORD God of Israel, There is an accursed thing in the midst of thee, O Israel: thou canst not stand before thine enemies, until ye take away the accursed thing from among you.** In the morning therefore ye shall be brought according to your tribes: and it shall be, that the tribe which the LORD taketh shall come according to the families thereof; and the family which the LORD shall take shall come by households; and the household which the LORD shall take shall come man by man. **And it shall be, that he that is taken with the accursed thing shall be burnt with fire, he and all that he hath:** because he hath transgressed the covenant of the LORD, and because he hath wrought folly in Israel. So Joshua rose up early in the morning, and brought Israel by their tribes; and the tribe of Judah was taken: And he brought the family of Judah; and he took the family of the Zarhites: and he brought the family of the Zarhites man by man; and Zabdi was taken: And he brought his household man by man; and Achan, the son of Carmi, the son of Zabdi, the son of Zerah, of the tribe of Judah, was taken. And Joshua said unto Achan, My son, give, I pray thee, glory to the LORD God of Israel, and make confession unto him; and tell me now what thou hast done; hide it not from me. And Achan answered Joshua, and said, Indeed I have sinned against the LORD God of Israel, and thus and thus have I done: When I saw among the spoils a goodly Babylonish garment, and two hundred shekels of silver, and a wedge of gold of fifty shekels weight, then I coveted them, and took them; and, behold, they are hid in the earth in the midst of my tent, and the silver under it. So Joshua sent messengers, and they ran unto the tent; and, behold, it was hid in his tent, and the silver under it. And they took them out of the midst of the tent, and brought them unto Joshua, and unto all the children of Israel, and laid them out before the LORD. **And Joshua, and all Israel with him, took Achan the son of Zerah, and the silver, and the garment, and the wedge of gold, and his sons, and his daughters, and his oxen, and his asses, and his sheep, and his tent, and all that he had: and they brought them unto the valley of Achor.** And Joshua said, Why hast thou troubled us? the LORD shall trouble thee this day. **And all Israel stoned him with stones, and burned them with fire, after they had stoned them with stones.** And they raised over him a great heap of stones unto this day. **So the LORD turned from the fierceness of his anger.** Wherefore the name of that place was called, The valley of Achor, unto this day.

Joshua 8:1-35 And the LORD said unto Joshua, Fear not, neither be thou dismayed: take all the people of war with thee, and arise, go up to Ai: see, I have given into thy hand the king of Ai, and his people, and his city, and his land: And thou shalt do to Ai and her king as thou didst unto Jericho and her king: only the spoil thereof, and the cattle thereof, shall ye take for a prey unto yourselves: lay thee an ambush for the city behind it. So Joshua arose, and all the people of war, to go up against Ai: and Joshua chose out thirty thousand mighty men of valour, and sent them away by night. And he commanded them, saying, Behold, ye shall lie in wait against the city, even behind the city: go not very far from the city, but be ye all ready: And I, and all the people that are with me, will approach unto the city: and it shall come to pass, when they come out against us, as at the first, that we will flee before them, (For they will come out after us) till we have drawn them from the city; for they will say, They flee before us, as at the first: therefore we will flee before them. Then ye shall rise up from the ambush, and seize upon the city: for the LORD your God will deliver it into your hand. And it shall be, when ye have taken the city, that ye shall set the city on fire: according to the commandment of the LORD shall ye do. See, I have commanded you. Joshua therefore sent them forth: and they went to lie in ambush, and abode between Bethel and Ai, on the west side of Ai: but Joshua lodged that night among the people. And Joshua rose up early in the morning, and numbered the people, and went up, he and the elders of Israel, before the people to Ai. And all the people, even the people of war that were with him, went up, and drew nigh, and came before the city, and pitched on the north side of Ai: now there was a valley between them and Ai. And he took about five thousand men, and set them to lie in ambush between Bethel and Ai, on the west side of the city. And when they had set the people, even all the host that was on the north of the city, and their liers in wait on the west of the city, Joshua went that night into the midst of the valley. And it came to pass, when the king of Ai saw it, that they hasted and rose up early, and the men of the city went out against Israel to battle, he and all his people, at a time appointed, before the plain; but he wist not that there were liers in ambush against him behind the city. And Joshua and all Israel made as if they were beaten before them, and fled by the way of the wilderness. And all the people that were in Ai were called together to pursue after them: and they pursued after Joshua, and were drawn away from the city. And there was not a man left in Ai or Bethel, that went not out after Israel: and they left the city open, and pursued after Israel. **And the LORD said unto Joshua, Stretch out the spear that is in thy hand toward Ai; for I will give it into thine hand. And Joshua stretched out the spear that he had in his hand toward the city.** And the ambush arose quickly out of their place, and they ran as soon as he had stretched out his hand: and they entered into the city, and took it, and hasted and set the city on fire. And when the men of Ai looked behind them, they saw, and, behold, the smoke of the city ascended up to heaven, and they had no power to flee this way or that way: and the people that fled to the wilderness turned back upon the pursuers. And when Joshua and all Israel saw that the ambush had taken the city, and that the smoke of the city ascended, then they turned again, and slew the men of Ai. And the other issued out of the city against them; so they were in the midst of Israel, some on this side, and some on that side: and they smote them, so that they let none of them remain or escape. And the king of Ai they took alive, and brought him to Joshua. And it came to pass, when Israel had made an end of slaying all the inhabitants of Ai in the field, in the wilderness wherein they chased them, and when they were all fallen on the edge of the sword, until they were consumed, that all the Israelites returned unto Ai, and smote it with the edge of the sword. **And so it was, that all that fell that day, both of men and women, were twelve thousand, even all the men of Ai. For Joshua drew not his hand back, wherewith he stretched out the spear, until he had utterly destroyed all the inhabitants of Ai.** Only the cattle and the spoil of that city Israel took for a prey unto themselves, according unto the word of the LORD which he commanded Joshua. And Joshua burnt Ai, and made it an heap for ever, even a desolation unto this day. And the king of Ai he hanged on a tree until eventide: and as soon as the sun was down, Joshua commanded that they should take his carcase down from the tree, and cast it at the entering of the gate of the city, and raise thereon a great heap of stones, that remaineth unto this day. Then Joshua built an altar unto the LORD God of Israel in mount Ebal, As Moses the servant of the LORD commanded the children of Israel, as it is written in the book of the law of Moses, an altar of whole stones, over which no man hath lift up any iron: and they offered thereon burnt offerings unto the LORD, and sacrificed peace offerings. And he wrote there upon the stones a copy of the law of Moses, which he wrote in the presence of the children of Israel. And all Israel, and their elders, and officers, and their judges, stood on this side the ark and on that side before the priests the Levites, which bare the ark of the covenant of the LORD, as well the stranger, as he that was born among them; half of them over against mount Gerizim, and half of them over against mount Ebal; as Moses the servant of the LORD had commanded before, that they should bless the people of Israel. **And afterward he read all the words of the law, the blessings and cursings, according to all that is written in the book of the law. There was not a word of all that Moses commanded, which Joshua read not before all the congregation of Israel, with the women, and the little ones, and the strangers that were conversant among them.**

Joshua 10:1-43 Now it came to pass, when Adonizedec king of Jerusalem had heard how Joshua had taken Ai, and had utterly destroyed it; as he had done to Jericho and her king, so he had done to Ai and her king; and how the inhabitants of Gibeon had made peace with Israel, and were among them; That they feared greatly, because Gibeon was a great city, as one of the royal cities, and because it was greater than Ai, and all the men thereof were mighty. Wherefore Adonizedec king of Jerusalem, sent unto Hoham king of Hebron, and unto Piram king of Jarmuth, and unto Japhia king of Lachish, and unto Debir king of Eglon, saying, Come up unto me, and help me, that we may smite Gibeon: for it hath made peace with Joshua and with the children of Israel. Therefore the five kings of the Amorites, the king of Jerusalem, the king of Hebron, the king of Jarmuth, the king of Lachish, the king of Eglon, gathered themselves together, and went up, they and all their hosts, and encamped before Gibeon, and made war against it. And the men of Gibeon sent unto Joshua to the camp to Gilgal, saying, Slack not thy hand from thy servants; come up to us quickly, and save us, and help us: for all the kings of the Amorites that dwell in the mountains are gathered together against us. So Joshua ascended from Gilgal, he, and all the people of war with him, and all the mighty men of valour. **And the LORD said unto Joshua, Fear them not: for I have delivered them into thine hand; there shall not a man of them stand before thee.** Joshua therefore came unto them suddenly, and went up from Gilgal all night. And the LORD discomfited them before Israel, and slew them with a great slaughter at Gibeon, and chased them along the way that goeth up to Bethhoron, and smote them to Azekah, and unto Makkedah. And it came to pass, as they fled from before Israel, and were in the going down to Bethhoron, that **the LORD cast down great stones from heaven upon them unto Azekah, and they died: they were more which died with hailstones than they whom the children of Israel slew with the sword.** Then spake Joshua to the LORD in the day when the LORD delivered up the Amorites before the children of Israel, and he said in the sight of Israel, Sun, stand thou still upon Gibeon; and thou, Moon, in the valley of Ajalon. **And the sun stood still, and the moon stayed, until the people had avenged themselves upon their enemies.** Is not this written in the book of Jasher? So the sun stood still in the midst of heaven, and hasted not to go down about a whole day. **And there was no day like that before it or after it, that the LORD hearkened unto the voice of a man: for the LORD fought for Israel.** And Joshua returned, and all Israel with him, unto the camp to Gilgal. But these five kings fled, and hid themselves in a cave at Makkedah. And it was told Joshua, saying, The five kings are found hid in a cave at Makkedah. And Joshua said, Roll great stones upon the mouth of the cave, and set men by it for to keep them: And stay ye not, but pursue after your enemies, and smite the hindmost of them; suffer them not to enter into their cities: for the LORD your God hath delivered them into your hand. And it came to pass, when Joshua and the children of Israel had made an end of slaying them with a very great slaughter, till they were consumed, that the rest which remained of them entered into fenced cities. And all the people returned to the camp to Joshua at Makkedah in peace: none moved his tongue against any of the children of Israel. Then said Joshua, Open the mouth of the cave, and bring out those five kings unto me out of the cave. And they did so, and brought forth those five kings unto him out of the cave, the king of Jerusalem, the king of Hebron, the king of Jarmuth, the king of Lachish, and the king of Eglon. And it came to pass, when they brought out those kings unto Joshua, that Joshua called for all the men of Israel, and said unto the captains of the men of war which went with him, Come near, put your feet upon the necks of these kings. And they came near, and put their feet upon the necks of them. And Joshua said unto them, Fear not, nor be dismayed, be strong and of good courage: for thus shall the LORD do to all your enemies against whom ye fight. And afterward Joshua smote them, and slew them, and hanged them on five trees: and they were hanging upon the trees until the evening. And it came to pass at the time of the going down of the sun, that Joshua commanded, and they took them down off the trees, and cast them into the cave wherein they had been hid, and laid great stones in the cave's mouth, which remain until this very day. And that day Joshua took Makkedah, and smote it with the edge of the sword, and the king thereof he **utterly destroyed**, them, and all the souls that were therein; he let none remain: and he did to the king of Makkedah as he did unto the king of Jericho. Then Joshua passed from Makkedah, and all Israel with him, unto Libnah, and fought against Libnah: And the LORD delivered it also, and the king thereof, into the hand of Israel; and he smote it with the edge of the sword, and all the souls that were therein; he let none remain in it; but did unto the king thereof as he did unto the king of Jericho. And Joshua passed from Libnah, and all Israel with him, unto Lachish, and encamped against it, and fought against it: And the LORD delivered Lachish into the hand of Israel, which took it on the second day, and smote it with the edge of the sword, and all the souls that were therein, according to all that he had done to Libnah. Then Horam king of Gezer came up to help Lachish; and Joshua smote him and his people, until he had left him none remaining. And from Lachish Joshua passed unto Eglon, and all Israel with him; and they encamped against it, and fought against it: And they took it on that day, and smote it with the edge of the sword, and all the souls that were therein he **utterly destroyed** that day, according to all that he had done to Lachish. And Joshua went up from Eglon, and all Israel with him, unto Hebron; and they fought against it: And they took it, and smote it with the edge of the sword, and the king thereof, and all the cities thereof, and all the souls that were therein; he left none remaining, according to all that he had done to Eglon; but **destroyed it utterly**, and all the souls that were therein. And Joshua returned, and all Israel with him, to Debir; and fought against it: And he took it, and the king thereof, and all the cities thereof; and they smote them with the edge of the sword, and **utterly destroyed** all the souls that were therein; he left none remaining: as he had done to Hebron, so he did to Debir, and to the king thereof; as he had done also to Libnah, and to her king. So Joshua smote all the country of the hills, and of the south, and of the vale, and of the springs, and all their kings: he left none remaining, but **utterly destroyed** all that breathed, as the Lord God of Israel commanded. And Joshua smote them from Kadeshbarnea even unto Gaza, and all the country of Goshen, even unto Gibeon. And all these kings and their land did Joshua take at one time, **because the Lord God of Israel fought for Israel.** And Joshua returned, and all Israel with him, unto the camp to Gilgal.

Joshua 11:1-23 And it came to pass, when Jabin king of Hazor had heard those things, that he sent to Jobab king of Madon, and to the king of Shimron, and to the king of Achshaph, And to the kings that were on the north of the mountains, and of the plains south of Chinneroth, and in the valley, and in the borders of Dor on the west, And to the Canaanite on the east and on the west, and to the Amorite, and the Hittite, and the Perizzite, and the Jebusite in the mountains, and to the Hivite under Hermon in the land of Mizpeh. And they went out, they and all their hosts with them, much people, even as the sand that is upon the sea shore in multitude, with horses and chariots very many. And when all these kings were met together, they came and pitched together at the waters of Merom, to fight against Israel. **And the Lord said unto Joshua, Be not afraid because of them:** for to morrow about this time will I

70

deliver them up all slain before Israel: thou shalt hough their horses, and burn their chariots with fire. So Joshua came, and all the people of war with him, against them by the waters of Merom suddenly; and they fell upon them. And the LORD delivered them into the hand of Israel, who smote them, and chased them unto great Zidon, and unto Misrephothmaim, and unto the valley of Mizpeh eastward; and they smote them, until they left them none remaining. And Joshua did unto them as the LORD bade him: he houghed their horses, and burnt their chariots with fire. And Joshua at that time turned back, and took Hazor, and smote the king thereof with the sword: for Hazor beforetime was the head of all those kingdoms. And they smote all the souls that were therein with the edge of the sword, **utterly destroying** them: there was not any left to breathe: and he burnt Hazor with fire. And all the cities of those kings, and all the kings of them, did Joshua take, and smote them with the edge of the sword, and he **utterly destroyed** them, as Moses the servant of the LORD commanded. But as for the cities that stood still in their strength, Israel burned none of them, save Hazor only; that did Joshua burn. And all the spoil of these cities, and the cattle, the children of Israel took for a prey unto themselves; but every man they smote with the edge of the sword, until they had destroyed them, neither left they any to breathe. As the LORD commanded Moses his servant, so did Moses command Joshua, and so did Joshua; he left nothing undone of all that the LORD commanded Moses. So Joshua took all that land, the hills, and all the south country, and all the land of Goshen, and the valley, and the plain, and the mountain of Israel, and the valley of the same; Even from the mount Halak, that goeth up to Seir, even unto Baalgad in the valley of Lebanon under mount Hermon: and all their kings he took, and smote them, and slew them. Joshua made war a long time with all those kings. There was not a city that made peace with the children of Israel, save the Hivites the inhabitants of Gibeon: all other they took in battle. **For it was of the LORD to harden their hearts, that they should come against Israel in battle, that he might destroy them utterly, and that they might have no favour, but that he might destroy them, as the LORD commanded Moses.** And at that time came Joshua, and cut off the Anakims from the mountains, from Hebron, from Debir, from Anab, and from all the mountains of Judah, and from all the mountains of Israel: Joshua **destroyed them utterly** with their cities. There was none of the Anakims left in the land of the children of Israel: only in Gaza, in Gath, and in Ashdod, there remained. **So Joshua took the whole land, according to all that the LORD said unto Moses; and Joshua gave it for an inheritance unto Israel according to their divisions by their tribes. And the land rested from war.**

<u>**Numbers 16:1-35**</u> Now Korah, the son of Izhar, the son of Kohath, the son of Levi, and Dathan and Abiram, the sons of Eliab, and On, the son of Peleth, sons of Reuben, took men: **And they rose up before Moses, with certain of the children of Israel, two hundred and fifty princes of the assembly, famous in the congregation, men of renown:** And they gathered themselves together against Moses and against Aaron, and said unto them, Ye take too much upon you, seeing all the congregation are holy, every one of them, and the LORD is among them: wherefore then lift ye up yourselves above the congregation of the LORD? And when Moses heard it, he fell upon his face: And he spake unto Korah and unto all his company, saying, Even to morrow **the LORD will shew who are his, and who is holy**; and will cause him to come near unto him: even him whom he hath chosen will he cause to come near unto him. This do; Take you censers, Korah, and all his company; And put fire therein, and put incense in them before the LORD to morrow: and it shall be that the man whom the LORD doth choose, he shall be holy: ye take too much upon you, ye sons of Levi. And Moses said unto Korah, Hear, I pray you, ye sons of Levi: Seemeth it but a small thing unto you, that the God of Israel hath separated you from the congregation of Israel, to bring you near to himself to do the service of the tabernacle of the LORD, and to stand before the congregation to minister unto them? And he hath brought thee near to Him, and all thy brethren the sons of Levi with thee: and seek ye the priesthood also? For which cause both thou and all thy company are gathered together against the LORD: and what is Aaron, that ye murmur against him? And Moses sent to call Dathan and Abiram, the sons of

Eliab: which said, We will not come up: Is it a small thing that thou hast brought us up out of a land that floweth with milk and honey, to kill us in the wilderness, except thou make thyself altogether a prince over us? Moreover thou hast not brought us into a land that floweth with milk and honey, or given us inheritance of fields and vineyards: wilt thou put out the eyes of these men? we will not come up. And Moses was very wroth, and said unto the LORD, Respect not thou their offering: I have not taken one ass from them, neither have I hurt one of them. And Moses said unto Korah, Be thou and all thy company before the LORD, thou, and they, and Aaron, to morrow: And take every man his censer, and put incense in them, and bring ye before the LORD every man his censer, **two hundred and fifty censers**; thou also, and Aaron, each of you his censer. And they took every man his censer, and put fire in them, and laid incense thereon, and stood in the door of the tabernacle of the congregation with Moses and Aaron. And Korah gathered all the congregation against them unto the door of the tabernacle of the congregation: and the glory of the LORD appeared unto all the congregation.   And the LORD spake unto Moses and unto Aaron, saying, Separate yourselves from among this congregation, that I may consume them in a moment. And they fell upon their faces, and said, O God, the God of the spirits of all flesh, shall one man sin, and wilt thou be wroth with all the congregation? And the Lord spake unto Moses, saying, Speak unto the congregation, saying, Get you up from about the tabernacle of Korah, Dathan, and Abiram. And Moses rose up and went unto Dathan and Abiram; and the elders of Israel followed him. And he spake unto the congregation, saying, Depart, I pray you, from the tents of these wicked men, and touch nothing of their's, lest ye be consumed in all their sins. So they gat up from the tabernacle of Korah, Dathan, and Abiram, on every side: and Dathan and Abiram came out, and stood in the door of their tents, and their wives, and their sons, and their little children. And Moses said, Hereby ye shall know that the LORD hath sent me to do all these works; for I have not done them of mine own mind. If these men die the common death of all men, or if they be visited after the visitation of all men; then the LORD hath not sent me. **But if the LORD make a new**

73

thing, and the earth open her mouth, and swallow them up, with all that appertain unto them, and they go down quick into the pit; then ye shall understand that these men have provoked the LORD. And it came to pass, as he had made an end of speaking all these words, that the ground clave asunder that was under them: And the earth opened her mouth, and swallowed them up, and their houses, and all the men that appertained unto Korah, and all their goods. They, and all that appertained to them, went down alive into the pit, and the earth closed upon them: and they perished from among the congregation. And all Israel that were round about them fled at the cry of them: for they said, Lest the earth swallow us up also. And there came out a fire from the LORD, and consumed the two hundred and fifty men that offered incense.

Numbers 16: 41-50 But on the morrow all the congregation of the children of Israel murmured against Moses and against Aaron, saying, Ye have killed the people of the LORD. And it came to pass, when the congregation was gathered against Moses and against Aaron, that they looked toward the tabernacle of the congregation: and, behold, the cloud covered it, and the glory of the LORD appeared. And Moses and Aaron came before the tabernacle of the congregation. And the LORD spake unto Moses, saying, Get you up from among this congregation, that I may consume them as in a moment. And they fell upon their faces. And Moses said unto Aaron, Take a censer, and put fire therein from off the altar, and put on incense, and go quickly unto the congregation, and make an atonement for them: for there is wrath gone out from the LORD; the plague is begun. And Aaron took as Moses commanded, and ran into the midst of the congregation; and, behold, the plague was begun among the people: and he put on incense, and made an atonement for the people. And he stood between the dead and the living; and the plague was stayed. **Now they that died in the plague were fourteen thousand and seven hundred, beside them that died about the matter of Korah.** And Aaron returned unto Moses unto the door of the tabernacle of the congregation: and the plague was stayed.

1-Corinthians 16:2 Upon the first day of the week let every one of you lay by him in store, **as God hath prospered him,** that there be no gatherings when I come.

Leviticus 27:30-34 And all the tithe of the land, whether of the seed of the land, or of the fruit of the tree, is the LORD's: **it is holy unto the LORD.** And if a man will at all redeem ought of his tithes, he shall add thereto the fifth part thereof. And concerning the tithe of the herd, or of the flock, even of whatsoever passeth under the rod, **the tenth shall be holy unto the LORD. He shall not search whether it be good or bad, neither shall he change it: and if he change it at all, then both it and the change thereof shall be holy**; it shall not be redeemed.   These are the commandments, which the LORD commanded Moses for the children of Israel in Mount Sinai.

Malachi 3:8-10 Will a man rob God? Bring ye all the tithes into the storehouse, that there may be meat in mine house, and prove me now herewith, saith the Lord of hosts, if I will not open you the windows of Heaven, and pour you out a blessing, that there shall not be room enough to receive it.

2-Corinthians 9:6-7 He which soweth sparingly shall reap also sparingly; and he which soweth bountifully shall reap also bountifully. Every man according as he purposeth in his heart, so let him give; not grudgingly, or of necessity; for God loveth a cheerful giver.

1-Timothy 6:10-11 For the *love of* money is the root of all evil: which while some coveted after, they have erred from the faith, and pierced themselves through with many sorrows. But thou, O man of God, flee these things; and follow after righteousness, godliness, faith, love, patience, meekness. **(Note that *money* is not the root of all evil, but the *love of* money is the root of all evil.)**

Matthew 5:42 Give to him that asketh thee, and from him that would borrow of thee turn not thou away.

Acts 20:35 Jesus said It is more blessed to give than to receive.

Exodus 22:25 If you lend money to any of My people who are poor among you, you shall not be like a moneylender to him; you shall not charge him interest.

Deuteronomy 23:20 To a foreigner you may charge interest, but to your brother you shall not charge interest, that the Lord may bless you.

Acts 5:1-10 But a certain man named Ananias, with Sapphira his wife, sold a possession, And kept back part of the price, his wife also being privy to it, and brought a certain part, and laid it at the apostles' feet. But Peter said, Ananias, why hath Satan filled thine heart to lie to the Holy Ghost, and to keep back part of the price of the land? Whiles it remained, was it not thine own? and after it was sold, was it not in thine own power? why hast thou conceived this thing in thine heart? thou hast not lied unto men, but unto God. And Ananias hearing these words fell down, and gave up the ghost: and great fear came on all them that heard these things. And the young men arose, wound him up, and carried him out, and buried him. And it was about the space of three hours after, when his wife, not knowing what was done, came in. And Peter answered unto her, Tell me whether ye sold the land for so much? And she said, Yea, for so much. Then Peter said unto her, How is it that ye have agreed together to tempt the Spirit of the Lord? behold, the feet of them which have buried thy husband are at the door, and shall carry thee out. Then fell she down straightway at his feet, and yielded up the ghost: and the young men came in, and found her dead, and, carrying her forth, buried her by her husband.

Proverbs 3:27-28 **Withhold not good from them to whom it is due, when it is in the power of thine hand to do it.** Say not unto thy neighbour, Go, and come again, and tomorrow I will give; when thou hast it by thee.

Luke 1:4-8, 11-20, 26-64 There was in the days of Herod, the king of Judaea, a certain priest named Zacharias, of the course of Abia: and his wife was of the daughters of Aaron, and her name was Elisabeth. **And they were both righteous before God, walking in all the commandments and ordinances of the Lord blameless. And they had no child, because that Elisabeth was barren, and they both were now well stricken in years.** And it came to pass, that while he executed the priest's office before God in the order of his course, And there appeared unto him an angel of the Lord standing on the right side of the altar of incense. And when Zacharias saw him, he was troubled, and fear fell upon him. **But the angel said unto him, Fear not, Zacharias: for thy prayer is heard; and thy wife Elisabeth shall bear thee a son, and thou shalt call his name John.** And thou shalt have joy and gladness; and many shall rejoice at his birth. For he shall be great in the sight of the Lord, and shall drink neither wine nor strong drink; and he shall be filled with the Holy Ghost, even from his mother's womb. And many of the children of Israel shall he turn to the Lord their God. And he shall go before him in the spirit and power of Elias, to turn the hearts of the fathers to the children, and the disobedient to the wisdom of the just; to make ready a people prepared for the Lord. And Zacharias said unto the angel, Whereby shall I know this? for I am an old man, and my wife well stricken in years. And the angel answering said unto him, **I am Gabriel**, that stand in the presence of God; and am sent to speak unto thee, and to shew thee these glad tidings. And, behold, **thou shalt be dumb, and not able to speak, until the day that these things shall be performed, because thou believest not my words,** which shall be fulfilled in their season. And in the sixth month the angel Gabriel was sent from God unto a city of Galilee, named Nazareth, To a virgin espoused to a man whose name was Joseph, of the house of David; and the virgin's name was Mary. And the angel came in unto her, and said, Hail, thou that art highly favoured, the Lord is with thee: blessed art thou among

77

women. And when she saw him, she was troubled at his saying, and cast in her mind what manner of salutation this should be. And the angel said unto her, Fear not, Mary: for thou hast found favour with God. And, behold, **thou shalt conceive in thy womb, and bring forth a son, and shalt call his name JESUS.** He shall be great, and shall be called the Son of the Highest: and the Lord God shall give unto him the throne of his father David: And he shall reign over the house of Jacob for ever; and of his kingdom there shall be no end. Then said Mary unto the angel, How shall this be, seeing I know not a man? And the angel answered and said unto her, The Holy Ghost shall come upon thee, and the power of the Highest shall overshadow thee: therefore also that holy thing which shall be born of thee shall be called the Son of God. And, behold, thy cousin Elisabeth, she hath also conceived a son in her old age: and this is the sixth month with her, who was called barren. **For with God nothing shall be impossible.** And Mary said, Behold the handmaid of the Lord; be it unto me according to thy word. And the angel departed from her. And Mary arose in those days, and went into the hill country with haste, into a city of Juda; And entered into the house of Zacharias, and saluted Elisabeth. And it came to pass, that, when Elisabeth heard the salutation of Mary, the babe leaped in her womb; and Elisabeth was filled with the Holy Ghost: And she spake out with a loud voice, and said, Blessed art thou among women, and blessed is the fruit of thy womb. And whence is this to me, that the mother of my Lord should come to me? For, lo, as soon as the voice of thy salutation sounded in mine ears, the babe leaped in my womb for joy. And blessed is she that believed: for there shall be a performance of those things which were told her from the Lord. And Mary said, My soul doth magnify the Lord, And my spirit hath rejoiced in God my Saviour. For he hath regarded the low estate of his handmaiden: for, behold, from henceforth all generations shall call me blessed. For he that is mighty hath done to me great things; and holy is his name. And his mercy is on them that fear him from generation to generation. He hath shewed strength with his arm; he hath scattered the proud in the imagination of their hearts. He hath put down the mighty from their seats, and exalted them of low degree. He hath filled the hungry with

78

good things; and the rich he hath sent empty away. He hath helped his servant Israel, in remembrance of his mercy; As he spake to our fathers, to Abraham, and to his seed for ever. And Mary abode with her about three months, and returned to her own house. Now Elisabeth's full time came that she should be delivered; and she brought forth a son. And her neighbours and her cousins heard how the Lord had shewed great mercy upon her; and they rejoiced with her. And it came to pass, that on the eighth day they came to circumcise the child; and they called him Zacharias, after the name of his father. And his mother answered and said, Not so; but he shall be called John. And they said unto her, There is none of thy kindred that is called by this name. And they made signs to his father, how he would have him called. And he asked for a writing table, and wrote, saying, **His name is John.** And they marvelled all. **And his mouth was opened immediately, and his tongue loosed, and he spake, and praised God.**

(The following emphasizes that even though John's birth was foretold by an Angel, and even though John was the cousin of Jesus, and even though John was a just and holy man who baptized many souls, and even though he baptized Jesus the Son of God Himself, nevertheless, because there is no respect of persons, John's fate was to be beheaded unjustly at the whim of the king's wife and step daughter.)

<u>Mark 6:17-29</u> For Herod himself had sent forth and laid hold upon John, and bound him in prison for Herodias' sake, his brother Philip's wife: for he had married her. **For John had said unto Herod, It is not lawful for thee to have thy brother's wife. Therefore Herodias had a quarrel against him, and would have killed him; but she could not: For Herod feared John, knowing that he was a just man and an holy**, and observed him; and when he heard him, he did many things, and heard him gladly. And when a convenient day was come, that Herod on his birthday made a supper to his lords, high captains, and chief estates of Galilee; And when the daughter of the said Herodias came in, and danced, and pleased Herod and them that sat with him, the king said unto the damsel, Ask of me whatsoever thou wilt, and I will give it thee. And he sware

79

unto her, Whatsoever thou shalt ask of me, I will give it thee, unto the half of my kingdom. **And she went forth, and said unto her mother, What shall I ask? And she said, The head of John the Baptist.** And she came in straightway with haste unto the king, and asked, saying, I will that thou give me by and by in a charger the head of John the Baptist. And the king was exceeding sorry; yet for his oath's sake, and for their sakes which sat with him, he would not reject her. **And immediately the king sent an executioner, and commanded his head to be brought: and he went and beheaded him in the prison,** And brought his head in a charger, and gave it to the damsel: and the damsel gave it to her mother. And ...His disciples ...came and took up his corpse, and laid it in a tomb.

Philippians 2:9-10 Wherefore God also hath highly exalted Him, and given Him a name which is above every name: That **at the name of Jesus** every knee should bow, of things in Heaven, and things in earth, and things under the earth;

Acts 4:7-12 And when they had set them in the midst, they asked, By what power, or by what name, have ye done this? Then Peter, filled with the Holy Ghost, said unto them, Ye rulers of the people, and elders of Israel, If we this day be examined of the good deed done to the impotent man, by what means he is made whole; Be it known unto you all, and to all the people of Israel, **that by the name of Jesus Christ of Nazareth**, whom ye crucified, whom God raised from the dead, even by Him doth this man stand here before you whole. This is the stone which was set at nought of you builders, which is become the head of the corner. Neither is there salvation in any other: for **there is none other name under Heaven given among men, whereby we must be saved**.

John 14:1-9, 13 Let not your heart be troubled: ye believe in God, believe also in Me. **In my Father's house are many mansions: if it were not so, I would have told you. I go to prepare a place for you.** And if I go and prepare a place for you, I will come again, and receive you unto Myself; that where I am, there ye may be also. And whither I go ye know, and the way ye know. Thomas saith unto him, Lord, we know not whither thou goest; and how can we know the way? **Jesus saith unto him, I am the way, the truth, and the life: no man cometh unto the Father, but by Me.** If ye had known Me, ye should have known My Father also: and from henceforth ye know Him, and have seen Him. Philip saith unto Him, Lord, show us the Father, and it sufficeth us. Jesus saith unto him, Have I been so long time with you, and yet hast thou not known Me, Philip? **he that hath seen Me hath seen the Father;** and how sayest thou then, Show us the Father? **And**

81

whatsoever ye shall ask in My name, that will I do, that the Father may be glorified in the Son.

Matthew 9:11-13 And when the Pharisees saw it, they said unto his disciples, Why eateth your Master with publicans and sinners? Jesus said unto them, **They that be whole need not a physician, but they that are sick. for I am not come to call the righteous, but sinners to repentance.**

1-John 3:8 He that committeth sin is of the devil; for the devil sinneth from the beginning. **For this purpose the Son of God was manifested, that He might destroy the works of the devil.**

John 14:20-21, 26-28 At that day ye shall know that I am in My Father, and ye in Me, and I in you. He that hath My commandments, and keepeth them, he it is that loveth Me: and he that loveth Me shall be loved of my Father, and I will love him, and will manifest Myself to him. But **the Comforter, which is the Holy Ghost, whom the Father will send in My name, He shall teach you all things, and bring all things to your remembrance**, whatsoever I have said unto you. Peace I leave with you, My peace I give unto you: not as the world giveth, give I unto you. Let not your heart be troubled, neither let it be afraid. Ye have heard how I said unto you, I go away, and come again unto you. If ye loved Me, ye would rejoice, because I said, I go unto the Father: for **My Father is greater than I.**

Ephesians 1:17-23 That the God of our Lord Jesus Christ, the Father of glory, may give unto you the spirit of wisdom and revelation in the knowledge of Him: The eyes of your understanding being enlightened; that ye may know what is the hope of His calling, and what the riches of the glory of His inheritance in the saints, And what is the exceeding greatness of His power to us-ward who believe, according to the working of His mighty power, Which He wrought in **Christ**, when He raised Him from the dead, and set Him at His own right hand in the Heavenly places, **Far above all principality, and power, and might, and dominion, and every name that is named, not only in this world, but also in that which is to come:** And hath put all things under His feet, and gave Him to be the head over all things to the church, Which is His body, the fulness of Him that filleth all in all.

1-Corinthians 15:3-4, 22 For I delivered unto you first of all that which I also received, how that Christ died for our sins according to the scriptures; And that He was buried, and that He rose again the third day according to the scriptures: For as in Adam all die, even so in Christ shall all be made alive.

1-Timothy 1:14-15 And the grace of our Lord was exceeding abundant with faith and love which is in Christ Jesus. This is a faithful saying, and worthy of all acceptation, that Christ Jesus came into the world to save sinners; of whom I am chief.

John 15:1-8 I am the true vine, and My Father is the husbandman. Every branch in Me that beareth not fruit He taketh away: and every branch that beareth fruit, He purgeth it, that it may bring forth more fruit. Now ye are clean through the word which I have spoken unto you. Abide in Me, and I in you. As the branch cannot bear fruit of itself, except it abide in the vine; no more can ye, except ye abide in Me. I am the vine, ye are the branches: He that abideth in Me, and I in him, the same bringeth forth much fruit: for without Me ye can do nothing. If a man abide not in Me, he is cast forth as a branch, and is withered; and men gather them, and cast them into the fire, and they are burned. If ye abide in Me, and My words abide in you, ye shall ask what ye will, and it shall be done unto you. Herein is my Father glorified, that ye bear much fruit; so shall ye be My disciples.

Philippians 2:5-8 Let this mind be in you, which was also in Christ Jesus: Who, being in the form of God, thought it not robbery to be equal with God: But made Himself of no reputation, and took upon Him the form of a servant, and was made in the likeness of men: And being found in fashion as a man, he humbled himself, and became obedient unto death, even the death of the cross.

Hebrews 1:1-4 God, who at sundry times and in divers manners spake in time past unto the fathers by the prophets, Hath in these last days spoken unto us by his Son, whom He hath appointed heir of all things, by whom also He made the worlds; Who being the brightness of His glory, and **the express image of His person**, and upholding all things by the word of His power, when He had by Himself purged our sins, sat down on the right hand of the Majesty on high: Being made so much better than the angels, as He hath by inheritance obtained a more excellent name than they.

Proverbs 22:1 **A good name is rather to be chosen than great riches, and loving favour rather than silver and gold.**

Jeremiah 17:7 **Blessed is the man that trusteth in the Lord,** and whose hope the Lord is.

James 1:12 **Blessed is the man that endureth temptation:** for when he is tried, he shall receive the crown of life, which the Lord hath promised to them that love Him.

1-Corinthians 10:13 There hath no *temptation* taken you but such as is common to man: but **God is faithful**, who will not suffer you to be tempted above that ye are able; but will with the *temptation* also make a way to escape, that ye may be able to bear it. **(Note: People often say that "God will not put more on you than you can bear", but this scripture shows that God will not put more *temptation* on you than you can bear.)**

Psalm 1:1-2 **Blessed is the man that walketh not in the counsel of the ungodly, nor standeth in the way of sinners, nor sitteth in the seat of the scornful.** But his delight is in the law of the Lord; and in His law doth he meditate day and night.

Psalm 32:2 **Blessed is the man unto whom the Lord imputeth not iniquity**, and in whose spirit there is no guile.

Romans 4:8 **Blessed is the man to whom the Lord will not impute sin.**

Psalm 34:8 **Blessed is the man that trusteth in Him.**

Psalm 40:4 **Blessed is that man that maketh the Lord his trust, and respecteth not the proud**, nor such as turn aside to lies.

Psalm 65:4 **Blessed is the man whom thou choosest, and causest to approach unto thee,** that he may dwell in thy courts: we shall be satisfied with the goodness of thy house, even of thy holy temple.

Psalm 84:5 **Blessed is the man whose strength is in Thee**; in whose heart are the ways of them.

Psalm 84:12 **Blessed is the man that trusteth in Thee.**

Psalm 94:12 **Blessed is the man whom thou chastenest,** O Lord, and teachest him out of thy law;
Proverbs 8:34 **Blessed is the man that heareth me,** watching daily at My gates, waiting at the posts of My doors.

Isaiah 56:2 **Blessed is the man that doeth this,** and the Son of man that layeth hold on it; that keepeth the Sabbath from polluting it, and keepeth his hand from doing any evil.

Luke 6:21 **Blessed are ye that hunger now**: for ye shall be filled. Blessed are ye that weep now: for ye shall laugh.

Luke 6:22 **Blessed are ye, when men shall hate you, and when they shall separate you from their company, and shall reproach you, and cast out your name as evil**, for the Son of man's sake.

Psalm 41:1-3 **Blessed is he who considers the poor**; The Lord will deliver him in time of trouble. The LORD will preserve him and keep him alive, And he will be blessed on the earth; You will not deliver him to the will of his enemies. The LORD will strengthen him on his bed of illness; You will sustain him on his sickbed.

Luke 11:28 **Blessed are they that hear the word of God, and keep it**.

Luke 6:20 **Blessed are you poor**, for yours is the kingdom of God.

Matthew 5:1-2 And seeing the multitudes, He went up into a mountain: and when He was set, His disciples came unto Him: And He opened his mouth, and taught them, saying,

Matthew 5:3 **Blessed are the poor in spirit**: for theirs is the kingdom of Heaven.

Matthew 5:4 **Blessed are they that mourn**: for they shall be comforted.

Matthew 5:5 **Blessed are the meek**: for they shall inherit the earth.

Matthew 5:6 **Blessed are they which do hunger and thirst after righteousness**: for they shall be filled.

Matthew 5:7 **Blessed are the merciful**: for they shall obtain mercy.

Matthew 5:8 **Blessed are the pure in heart**: for they shall see God.

Matthew 5:9 **Blessed are the peacemakers**: for they shall be called the children of God.

Matthew 5:10 **Blessed are they which are persecuted for righteousness' sake**: for theirs is the kingdom of Heaven.

Matthew 5:11 **Blessed are ye, when men shall revile you, and persecute you, and shall say all manner of evil against you falsely,** for My sake.

Matthew 5:14-16 Ye are the light of the world. A city that is set on an hill cannot be hid. **Neither do men light a candle, and put it under a bushel,** but on a candlestick; and it giveth light unto all that are in the house. **Let your light so shine before men, that they may see your good works, and glorify your Father which is in Heaven.**

Matthew 5:17-20 Think not that I am come to destroy the law, or the prophets: I am not come to destroy, but to fulfil. For verily I say unto you, **Till Heaven and earth pass, one jot or one tittle shall in no wise pass from the law, till all be fulfilled.** Whosoever therefore shall break one of these least commandments, and shall teach men so, he shall be called the least in the kingdom of Heaven: but whosoever shall do and teach them, the same shall be called great in the kingdom of Heaven. For I say unto you, **That except your righteousness shall exceed the righteousness of the scribes and Pharisees, ye shall in no case enter into the kingdom of Heaven.**

Matthew 5:21-26 Ye have heard that it was said of them of old time, Thou shalt not kill; and whosoever shall kill shall be in danger of the judgment: But I say unto you, That **whosoever is angry with his brother without a cause shall be in danger of the judgment**: and whosoever shall say to his brother, Raca, shall be in danger of the council: but **whosoever shall say, Thou fool, shall be in danger of hell fire**. Therefore if thou bring thy gift to the altar, and there rememberest that thy brother hath ought against thee; Leave there thy gift before the altar, and go thy way; first be reconciled to thy brother, and then come and offer thy gift. **Agree with thine adversary quickly**, whiles thou art in the way with him; lest at any time the adversary deliver thee to the judge, and the judge deliver thee to the officer, and thou be cast into prison.   Verily I say unto thee, Thou shalt by no means come out thence, till thou hast paid the uttermost farthing.

Matthew 5:27-28 Ye have heard that it was said by them of old time, Thou shalt not commit adultery: But I say unto you, That **whosoever looketh on a woman to lust after her hath committed adultery with her already in his heart.**

Matthew 5:29-30 And if thy right eye offend thee, pluck it out, and cast it from thee: for it is profitable for thee that one of thy members should perish, and not that thy whole body should be cast into hell. And if thy right hand offend thee, cut it off, and cast it from thee: for **it is profitable for**

thee that one of thy members should perish, and not that thy whole body should be cast into hell.

Matthew 5:31-32 It hath been said, Whosoever shall put away his wife, let him give her a writing of divorcement: But I say unto you, That whosoever shall put away his wife, **saving for the cause of fornication**, causeth her to commit adultery: and whosoever shall marry her that is divorced committeth adultery.

Matthew 5:33-37 Again, ye have heard that it hath been said by them of old time, Thou shalt not forswear thyself, but shalt perform unto the Lord thine oaths: But I say unto you, **Swear not at all; neither by Heaven; for it is God's throne: Nor by the earth; for it is His footstool: neither by Jerusalem; for it is the city of the great King. Neither shalt thou swear by thy head, because thou canst not make one hair white or black.   But let your communication be, Yea, yea; Nay, nay: for whatsoever is more than these cometh of evil.**

Matthew 5:38-39 Ye have heard that it hath been said, An eye for an eye, and a tooth for a tooth: But I say unto you, That ye resist not evil: but whosoever shall smite thee on thy right cheek, **turn to him the other also**.

Matthew 5:40 And if any man will sue thee at the law, and take away thy coat, let him have thy cloak also.

Matthew 5:41 And whosoever shall compel thee to go a mile, go with him twain.

Matthew 5:42 Give to him that asketh thee, and from him that would borrow of thee turn not thou away.

Matthew 5:43-48 Ye have heard that it hath been said, Thou shalt love thy neighbour, and hate thine enemy. But I say unto you, **Love your enemies, bless them that curse you, do good to them that hate you, and pray for them which despitefully use you, and persecute you; That ye may be the children of your Father which is in Heaven: for He maketh His sun to rise on the evil and on the**

good, and sendeth rain on the just and on the unjust. For if ye love them which love you, what reward have ye? do not even the publicans the same? And if ye salute your brethren only, what do ye more than others? do not even the publicans so? Be ye therefore perfect, even as your Father which is in Heaven is perfect.

Matthew 6:1-4 (when thou doest alms) Take heed that ye do not your alms before men, to be seen of them: otherwise ye have no reward of your Father which is in Heaven. Therefore when thou doest thine alms, do not sound a trumpet before thee, as the hypocrites do in the synagogues and in the streets, that they may have glory of men. Verily I say unto you, They have their reward. But when thou doest alms, let not thy left hand know what thy right hand doeth: That thine alms may be in secret: and thy Father which seeth in secret himself shall reward thee openly.

Matthew 6:5-8 (when thou prayest) And when thou prayest, thou shalt not be as the hypocrites are: for they love to pray standing in the synagogues and in the corners of the streets, that they may be seen of men. Verily I say unto you, They have their reward. But thou, when thou prayest, enter into thy closet, and when thou hast shut thy door, pray to thy Father which is in secret; and thy Father which seeth in secret shall reward thee openly. But when ye pray, use not vain repetitions, as the heathen do: for they think that they shall be heard for their much speaking. Be not ye therefore like unto them: for your Father knoweth what things ye have need of, before ye ask him.

Matthew 6:9-13 (the model prayer) After this manner therefore pray ye: Our Father which art in Heaven, Hallowed be thy name. Thy kingdom come, Thy will be done in earth, as it is in Heaven. Give us this day our daily bread. And forgive us our debts, as we forgive our debtors. And lead us not into temptation, but deliver us from evil: For thine is the kingdom, and the power, and the glory, for ever. Amen.

Matthew 6:14-15 (if you forgive or not forgive) For if ye forgive men their trespasses, your Heavenly Father will also forgive you: But if ye forgive not men their trespasses, neither will your Father forgive your trespasses.

Matthew 6:16-18 (when ye fast) Moreover when ye fast, be not, as the hypocrites, of a sad countenance: for they disfigure their faces, that they may appear unto men to fast. Verily I say unto you, They have their reward. But thou, when thou fastest, anoint thine head, and wash thy face; That thou appear not unto men to fast, but unto thy Father which is in secret: and thy Father, which seeth in secret, shall reward thee openly.

Matthew 6:19-21 (lay up treasures) Lay not up for yourselves treasures upon earth, where moth and rust doth corrupt, and where thieves break through and steal: But lay up for yourselves treasures in Heaven, where neither moth nor rust doth corrupt, and where thieves do not break through nor steal: For where your treasure is, there will your heart be also.

Matthew 6:22-24 (no man can serve two masters) The light of the body is the eye: if therefore thine eye be single, thy whole body shall be full of light. But if thine eye be evil, thy whole body shall be full of darkness. If therefore the light that is in thee be darkness, how great is that darkness! No man can serve two masters: for either he will hate the one, and love the other; or else he will hold to the one, and despise the other. Ye cannot serve God and mammon.

Matthew 6:25-34 (don't worry) Therefore I say unto you, Take no thought for your life, what ye shall eat, or what ye shall drink; nor yet for your body, what ye shall put on. Is not the life more than meat, and the body than raiment? Behold the fowls of the air: for they sow not, neither do they reap, nor gather into barns; yet your Heavenly Father feedeth them. Are ye not much better than they? **Which of you by taking thought can add one cubit unto his stature?** And why take ye thought for raiment? Consider the lilies of the field, how they grow; they toil not, neither do they spin: And yet I say unto you, That even Solomon in all his glory was not arrayed like one of these. Wherefore, if God so clothe the grass of the field, which to day is, and to morrow is cast into the oven, shall He not much more clothe you,   O ye of little faith?   **Therefore take no thought, saying, What shall we eat? or, What shall we drink? or, Wherewithal shall we be clothed?** (For after all these things do the Gentiles seek:) **for your Heavenly Father knoweth that ye have need of all these things.** But seek ye first the kingdom of God, and His righteousness; and all these things shall be added unto you. Take therefore no thought for the morrow: for the morrow shall take thought for the things of itself. Sufficient unto the day is the evil thereof.

Matthew 7:1-5 (judge fairly)   Judge not, that ye be not judged.   For with what judgment ye judge, ye shall be judged: and with what measure ye mete, it shall be measured to you again.   And why beholdest thou the mote that is in thy brother's eye, but considerest not the beam that is in thine own eye?   Or how wilt thou say to thy brother, Let me pull out the mote out of thine eye; and, behold, a beam is in thine own eye? Thou hypocrite, first cast out the beam out of thine own eye; and then shalt thou see clearly to cast out the mote out of thy brother's eye.

Matthew 7:7-12 (must ask) Ask, and it shall be given you; seek, and ye shall find; knock, and it shall be opened unto you: For every one that asketh receiveth; and he that seeketh findeth; and to him that knocketh it shall be opened. Or what man is there of you, whom if his son ask bread, will he give him a stone? Or if he ask a fish, will he give him a serpent? **If ye then, being evil, know how to give good gifts unto your children, how much more shall your Father which is in Heaven give good things to them that ask Him?**   Therefore all things whatsoever ye would that men should do to you, do ye even so to them: for this is the law and the prophets.

Matthew 7:13-23 (beware of false prophets) Enter ye in at the strait gate: for wide is the gate, and broad is the way, that leadeth to destruction, and many there be which go in thereat: Because strait is the gate, and narrow is the way, which leadeth unto life, and few there be that find it.

Beware of false prophets, which come to you in sheep's clothing, but inwardly they are ravening wolves. Ye shall know them by their fruits. Do men gather grapes of thorns, or figs of thistles? Even so every good tree bringeth forth good fruit; but a corrupt tree bringeth forth evil fruit. A good tree cannot bring forth evil fruit, neither can a corrupt tree bring forth good fruit. Every tree that bringeth not forth good fruit is hewn down, and cast into the fire. Wherefore by their fruits ye shall know them. **Not every one that saith unto Me, Lord, Lord, shall enter into the kingdom of Heaven; but he that doeth the will of My Father which is in Heaven.** Many will say to Me in that day, Lord, Lord, have we not prophesied in thy name? and in thy name have cast out devils? and in thy name done many wonderful works? And then will I profess unto them, I never knew you: depart from Me, ye that work iniquity.

Matthew 7:24-27 (house built upon a rock) Therefore whosoever heareth these sayings of Mine, and doeth them, I will liken him unto a wise man, which built his house upon a rock: And the rain descended, and the floods came, and the winds blew, and beat upon that house; and it fell not: for it was founded upon a rock. And every one that heareth these sayings of Mine, and doeth them not, shall be likened unto a foolish man, which built his house upon the sand: And the rain descended, and the floods came, and the winds blew, and beat upon that house; and it fell: and great was the fall of it. And it came to pass, when Jesus had ended these sayings, the people were astonished at His doctrine: For He taught them as one having authority, and not as the scribes.

Matthew 15:1-2, 10-12, 16-20 (unclean hands) Then came to Jesus scribes and Pharisees, which were of Jerusalem, saying, Why do thy disciples transgress the tradition of the elders? for they wash not their hands when they eat bread. And He called the multitude, and said unto them, Hear, and understand: Not that which goeth into the mouth defileth a man; but that which cometh out of the mouth, this defileth a man. Then came his disciples, and said unto Him, Knowest thou that the Pharisees were offended, after they heard this saying? And Jesus said, Are ye also yet without understanding? Do not ye yet understand, that whatsoever entereth in at the mouth goeth into the belly, and is cast out into the draught? But those things which proceed out of the mouth come forth from the heart; and they defile the man. For out of the heart proceed evil thoughts, murders, adulteries, fornications, thefts, false witness, blasphemies: These are the things which defile a man: **but to eat with unwashen hands defileth not a man.**

Matthew 10:28 And fear not them which kill the body, but are not able to kill the soul: but rather **fear him which is able to destroy both soul and body in hell.**

Matthew 10:32-33 Whosoever therefore shall confess Me before men, **him will I confess also before My Father which is in Heaven.** But whosoever shall deny Me before men, him will I also deny before My Father which is in Heaven.

Matthew 26:36-46 Then cometh Jesus with them unto a place called Gethsemane, and saith unto the disciples, Sit ye here, while I go and pray yonder. And He took with Him Peter and the two sons of Zebedee, and began to be sorrowful and very heavy. Then saith He unto them, My soul is exceeding sorrowful, even unto death: tarry ye here, and watch with Me. And He went a little farther, and fell on His face, and prayed, saying, O My Father, if it be possible, let this cup pass from Me: nevertheless not as I will, but as Thou wilt. And he cometh unto the disciples, and findeth them asleep, and saith unto Peter, **What, could ye not watch with Me one hour? Watch and pray, that ye enter not into temptation: the spirit indeed is willing, but the flesh is weak.** He went away again the second time, and prayed, saying, O My Father, if this cup may not pass away from Me, except I drink it, thy will be done. And He came and found them asleep again: for their eyes were heavy. And He left them, and went away again, and prayed the third time, saying the same. Then cometh He to His disciples, and saith unto them, Sleep on now, and take your rest: behold, the hour is at hand, and the Son of man is betrayed into the hands of sinners. Rise, let us be going: behold, he is at hand that doth betray Me.

Mark 10:35-40 And James and John, the sons of Zebedee, come unto Him, saying, Master, we would that Thou shouldest do for us whatsoever we shall desire. And He said unto them, What would ye that I should do for you? They said unto Him, **Grant unto us that we may sit, one on thy right hand, and the other on thy left hand, in thy glory.** But Jesus said unto them, Ye know not what ye ask: can ye drink of the cup that I drink of? and be baptized with the baptism that I am baptized with? And they said unto Him, We can. And Jesus said unto them, Ye shall indeed drink of the cup that I drink of; and with the baptism that I am baptized withal shall ye be baptized: But **to sit on My right hand and on My left hand is not Mine to give; but it shall be given to them for whom it is prepared.**

Mark 11:15-17 And they come to Jerusalem: and Jesus went into the temple, and began to cast out them that sold and bought in the temple, and overthrew the tables of the moneychangers, and the seats of them that sold doves; And would not suffer that any man should carry any vessel through the temple. And He taught, saying unto them, Is it not written, **My house shall be called of all nations the house of prayer?** but ye have made it a den of thieves.

Mark 12:41-44 And Jesus sat over against the treasury, and beheld how the people cast money into the treasury: and many that were rich cast in much. And there came a certain poor widow, and she threw in two mites, which make a farthing. And He called unto Him His disciples, and saith unto them, Verily I say unto you, That **this poor widow hath cast more in, than all they which have cast into the treasury: For all they did cast in of their abundance; but she of her want did cast in all that she had, even all her living.**

John 15:18-20, If the world hate you, ye know that it hated Me before it hated you. If ye were of the world, the world would love his own: but because ye are not of the world, but I have chosen you out of the world, therefore the world hateth you. Remember the word that I said unto you, The servant is not greater than his Lord. If they have persecuted Me, they will also persecute you; …………

James 3:3-12 Behold, we put bits in the horses' mouths, that they may obey us; and we turn about their whole body. Behold also the ships, which though they be so great, and are driven of fierce winds, yet are they turned about with a very small helm, whithersoever the governor listeth. Even so the tongue is a little member, and boasteth great things. Behold, how great a matter a little fire kindleth! And the tongue is a fire, a world of iniquity: so is the tongue among our members, that it defileth the whole body, and setteth on fire the course of nature; and it is set on fire of hell. For every kind of beasts, and of birds, and of serpents, and of things in the sea, is tamed, and hath been tamed of mankind: **But the tongue can no man tame; it is an unruly evil, full of deadly poison. Therewith bless we God, even the Father; and therewith curse we men, which are made after the similitude of God. Out of the same mouth proceedeth blessing and cursing. My brethren, these things ought not so to be.** Doth a fountain send forth at the same place sweet water and bitter? Can the fig tree, my brethren, bear olive berries? either a vine, figs? so can no fountain both yield salt water and fresh.

Matthew 12:36-37 But I say unto you, **That every idle word that men shall speak, they shall give account thereof in the day of judgment.** For by thy words thou shalt be justified, and by thy words thou shalt be condemned.

Colossians 3:8 **Put off** all these: **anger, filthy communication out of your mouth.**

Colossians 3:16 Let the word of Christ dwell in you richly in all wisdom; teaching and admonishing one another in Psalms and hymns and spiritual songs, singing with grace in your hearts to the Lord.

Colossians 4:6 Let your speech be always with grace, that ye may know how ye ought to answer every man.

Luke 9:23 And He said to them all, **If any man will come after Me, let him deny himself, and take up his cross daily, and follow Me.**

Matthew 23:8-12 But be not ye called Rabbi: for one is your Master, even Christ; and all ye are brethren. And **call no man your father upon the earth: for one is your Father, which is in Heaven.** Neither be ye called masters: for one is your Master, even Christ. But he that is greatest among you shall be your servant. And whosoever shall exalt himself shall be abased; and he that shall humble himself shall be exalted.

Ecclesiastes 10:12 The words of a wise man's mouth are gracious; but the lips of a fool will swallow up himself.

Romans 5:3-4 **We glory in tribulations also: knowing that tribulation worketh patience; and patience, experience; and experience, hope:**

Romans 12:15-16 Rejoice with them that do rejoice, and weep with them that weep. Be of the same mind one toward another. **Mind not high things, but condescend to men of low estate.** Be not wise in your own conceits.

Luke 14:8-11 Sit down in the lowest room. For whosoever exalteth himself shall be abased; & **he that humbleth himself shall be exalted**.

James 4:7-8 Submit yourselves therefore to God. **Resist the devil, and he will flee from you.** Draw nigh to God, and he will draw nigh to you. Cleanse your hands, ye sinners; and purify your hearts, ye double minded.

Philippians 2:3 In lowliness of mind, let each esteem others better than themselves.

1-Thessalonians 5:22 Abstain from all appearance of evil.

1-Thessalonians 5:26 Greet all the brethren with an holy kiss.

2-Corinthians 5:17 Therefore **if any man be in Christ, he is a new creature**: old things are passed away; behold, all things are become new.

Ephesians 5:1-2 **Be ye therefore followers of God**, as dear children; And walk in love, as Christ also hath loved us, and hath given Himself for us an offering and a sacrifice to God for a sweetsmelling savour.

Ephesians 5:6-7 **Let no man deceive you with vain words**: for because of these things cometh the wrath of God upon the children of disobedience. **Be not ye therefore partakers with them.**

Ephesians 5:11-12 And **have no fellowship with the unfruitful works of darkness**, but rather reprove them. **For it is a shame even to speak of those things which are done of them in secret.**

Ephesians 5:19-21 **Speaking to yourselves in psalms and hymns and spiritual songs, singing and making melody in your heart to the Lord; Giving thanks always for all things unto God and the Father in the name of our Lord Jesus Christ; Submitting yourselves one to another in the fear of God.**

1-Corinthians 5:9-13 I wrote unto you in an epistle not to company with fornicators: Yet not altogether with the fornicators of this world, or with the covetous, or extortioners, or with idolaters; for then must ye needs go out of the world. But now I have written unto you not to keep company, if any man that is called a brother be a fornicator, or covetous, or an idolator, or a railer, or a drunkard, or an extortioner; with such an one no not to eat. For what have I to do to judge them also that are without? do not ye judge them that are within? But them that are without God judgeth. **Therefore put away from among yourselves that wicked person.**

Titus 2:1-6 But speak thou the things which become sound doctrine: That the aged men be sober, grave, temperate, sound in faith, in charity, in patience. The aged women likewise, that they be in behaviour as becometh holiness, not false accusers, not given to much wine, teachers of good things; That they may teach the young women to be sober, to love their husbands, to love their children, To be discreet, chaste, keepers at home, good, obedient to their own husbands, that the word of God be not blasphemed. Young men likewise exhort to be sober minded.

Romans 12:1-13 I beseech you therefore, brethren, by the mercies of God, that ye present your bodies a living sacrifice, holy, acceptable unto God, which is your reasonable service. **And be not conformed to this world: but be ye transformed by the renewing of your mind, that ye may prove what is that good, and acceptable, and perfect, will of God.** For I say, through the grace given unto me, to every man that is among you, not to think of himself more highly than he ought to think; but to think soberly, according as God hath dealt to every man the measure of faith. For as we have many members in one body, and all members have not the same office: **So we, being many, are one body in Christ, and every one members one of another. Having then gifts differing according to the grace that is given to us, whether prophecy,** let us prophesy according to the proportion of faith; **Or ministry,** let us wait on our ministering: or he that teacheth, on teaching; **Or he that exhorteth,** on exhortation: **he that giveth,** let him do it with simplicity; **he that ruleth,** with diligence; **he that sheweth mercy,** with cheerfulness. Let love be without dissimulation. **Abhor that which is evil; cleave to that which is good. Be kindly affectioned one to another with brotherly love;** in honour preferring one another; Not slothful in business; fervent in spirit; serving the Lord; Rejoicing in hope; patient in tribulation; continuing instant in prayer; Distributing to the necessity of saints; given to hospitality.

Ezekiel 44:20 They shall neither shave their heads nor let their hair grow long, but they shall keep their hair well trimmed.

Hebrews 12:1-2 Let us run with patience the race that is set before us, **Looking unto** Jesus the author and finisher of our faith; **Who for the joy that was set before Him endured the cross, despising the shame, and is set down at the right hand of the throne of God.**

1-Timothy 2:1 I **exhort** therefore, that, first of all, supplications, prayers, intercessions, and giving of thanks, be made for all men;

1-Thessalonians 5:14-15 Now we **exhort** you, brethren, warn them that are unruly, comfort the feebleminded, support the weak, be patient toward all men. See that none render evil for evil unto any man; but ever follow that which is good, both among yourselves, and to all men.

Hebrews 3:13 But **exhort** one another daily, while it is called Today; lest any of you be hardened through the deceitfulness of sin.

Jude 1:1-3, 24-25 Jude, the servant of Jesus Christ, and brother of James, to them that are sanctified by God the Father, and preserved in Jesus Christ, and called: Mercy unto you, and peace, and love, be multiplied. Beloved, when I gave all diligence to write unto you of the common salvation, it was needful for me to write unto you, and exhort you that ye should earnestly contend for the faith which was once delivered unto the saints. **Now unto Him that is able to keep you from falling, and to present you faultless before the presence of His glory with exceeding joy, To the only wise God our Saviour, be glory and majesty, dominion and power, both now and ever. Amen.**

2-Corinthians 13:11-14 Finally, brethren, farewell. Be perfect, be of good comfort, be of one mind, live in peace; and the God of love and peace shall be with you. **Greet one another with an holy kiss.** All the saints salute you. **The grace of the Lord Jesus Christ, and the love of God, and the communion of the Holy Ghost, be with you all. Amen.**

Psalm 19:14 Let the words of my mouth, and the meditation of my heart, be acceptable in thy sight, O Lord, my strength, and my redeemer.

Philippians 4:8 Finally brethren, whatsoever things are true, whatsoever things are honest, whatsoever things are just, whatsoever things are pure, whatsoever things are lovely, whatsoever things are of good report, **if there be any virtue, and if there be any praise, think on these things.**

Proverbs 27:10 Thine own friend, and thy Father's friend, forsake not; neither go into thy brother's house in the day of thy calamity: for better is a neighbour that is near than a brother far off.

Ruth 1:16-17 And Ruth said, Intreat me not to leave thee, or to return from following after thee: **for whither thou goest, I will go; and where thou lodgest, I will lodge: thy people shall be my people, and thy God my God:** Where thou diest, will I die, and there will I be buried: the Lord do so to me, and more also, if ought but death part thee and me.

Proverbs 6:16-19 These seven (7) things doth the Lord hate: A proud look, a lying tongue, hands that shed innocent blood, an heart that deviseth wicked imaginations, feet that be swift in running to mischief, a false witness that speaketh lies, and he that soweth discord among brethren.

Ephesians 6:10-18 Finally, my brethren, be strong in the Lord, and in the power of His might. **Put on the whole amour of God,** that ye may be able to stand against the wiles of the devil; that ye may be able to withstand in the evil day; for we wrestle not against flesh and blood, but against principalities, against powers, against the rulers of the darkness of this world, against spiritual wickedness in high places. Stand therefore, having your loins girt about with truth, and having on the breastplate of righteousness, And your feet shod with the preparation of the gospel of peace, Above all, taking the shield of faith, wherewith ye shall be able to quench all the fiery darts of the wicked, And take the helmet of salvation, and take the sword of the Spirit, which is the word of God, Praying always...........

1-Thessalonians 5:8 But let us, who are the children of the day, be sober, putting on the breastplate of faith and love; and for an helmet, the hope of salvation.

Galatians 5:22-23 **The fruit of the Spirit** is love, joy, peace, longsuffering, gentleness, goodness, faith, Meekness, temperance:

Colossians 3:1-2, 12-14 If ye then be risen with Christ, seek those things which are above, where Christ sitteth on the right hand of God. **Set your affection on things above, not on things on the earth.** Put on therefore, as the elect of God, holy and beloved, bowels of mercies, kindness, humbleness of mind, meekness, longsuffering; Forbearing one another, and forgiving one another, And above all these things put on charity.

1-Timothy 6:11 Flee these things and follow after righteousness, Godliness, faith, love, patience, meekness.

2-Timothy 2:22 Flee also youthful lusts: but follow righteousness, faith, charity, peace, with them that call on the Lord out of a pure heart.

102

Ephesians 4:32 And be ye kind one to another, tenderhearted, **forgiving one another,** even as God for Christ's sake hath forgiven you.

Luke 17:3-4 Take heed to yourselves: If thy brother trespass against thee, rebuke him; and if he repent, **forgive** him. And if he trespass against thee seven times in a day, and seven times in a day turn again to thee, saying, I repent; thou shalt **forgive** him.

Luke 23:34 Father **forgive** them, for they know not what they do.

Mark 11:25-26 And when ye stand praying, **forgive**, if ye have ought against any: that your Father also which is in heaven may **forgive** you your trespasses. But if ye do not **forgive**, neither will your Father which is in heaven **forgive** your trespasses.

Matthew 18:21-22 Then came Peter to Him, and said, Lord, how oft shall my brother sin against me, and I **forgive** him? till seven times? Jesus saith unto him, I say not unto thee, Until seven times: but, Until seventy times seven.

Matthew 18:23-35 One was brought unto him which owed him ten thousand talents. Then the Lord of that servant was moved with compassion, and forgave him of the debt. But the same servant took his fellowservant who owed him an hundred pence by the throat, saying Pay me. Then his Lord said, Shouldest not thou also have had compassion and pity? And his Lord was wroth and delivered him to the tormenters. So likewise shall my Heavenly Father do also unto you, if ye from your hearts **forgive** not every one his brother their trespasses.

Ephesians 4:26-27 **Be ye angry, and sin not: let not the sun go down upon your wrath.** Neither give place to the devil.

103

Matthew 5:22 But I say unto you, That **whosoever is angry with his brother without a cause** shall be in danger of the judgment: but whosoever shall say, Thou fool, shall be in danger of hell fire.

Ecclesiastes 7:9 Be not hasty in thy spirit to be angry: for anger resteth in the bosom of fools.

James 1:19 Wherefore, my beloved brethren, let every man be swift to hear, slow to speak, **slow to wrath**:

Numbers 14:18 **The Lord is longsuffering**, and of great mercy, forgiving iniquity and transgression, and by no means clearing the guilty, **visiting the iniquity of the fathers upon the children unto the third and fourth generation**.

Luke 12:15-30   And he said unto them, Take heed, and **beware of covetousness**: for a man's life consisteth not in the abundance of the things which he possesseth. And he spake a parable unto them, saying, The ground of a certain rich man brought forth plentifully: And he thought within himself, saying, What shall I do, because I have no room where to bestow my fruits? And he said, This will I do: I will pull down my barns, and build greater; and there will I bestow all my fruits and my goods. And I will say to my soul, Soul, thou hast much goods laid up for many years; take thine ease, eat, drink, and be merry. But God said unto him, Thou fool, this night thy soul shall be required of thee: then whose shall those things be, which thou hast provided? So is he that layeth up treasure for himself, and is not rich toward God. And he said unto his disciples, Therefore I say unto you, Take no thought for your life, what ye shall eat; neither for the body, what ye shall put on. The life is more than meat, and the body is more than raiment. **Consider the ravens:** for they neither sow nor reap; which neither have storehouse nor barn; and God feedeth them: how much more are ye better than the fowls? And which of you with taking thought can add to his stature one cubit? If ye then be not able to do that thing which is least, why take ye thought for the rest? **Consider the lilies** how they grow: they toil not, they spin not; and yet I say unto you, that Solomon in all his glory was not arrayed like one of these. If then God so clothe the grass, which is to day in the field, and to morrow is cast into the oven; how much more will he clothe you, O ye of little faith? And seek not ye what ye shall eat, or what ye shall drink, neither be ye of doubtful mind. For all these things do the nations of the world seek after: and your Father knoweth that ye have need of these things.

Hebrews 13:5   Let your conversation be without **covetousness;** and be content with such things as ye have.

1-Timothy 6:8 And having food and raiment let us be therewith content.

Philippians 4:11 For in whatsoever state I am, I have learned therewith to be content.

1-Thessalonians 5:18 In every thing give thanks: for this is the will of God in Christ Jesus concerning you.

Psalm 118:24 This is the day which the LORD hath made; we will rejoice and be glad in it.

1-Timothy 4:1-5 Now the Spirit speaketh expressly, that **in the latter times some shall depart from the faith,** giving heed to seducing spirits, and doctrines of devils; Speaking lies in hypocrisy; having their conscience seared with a hot iron; Forbidding to marry, and **commanding to abstain from meats**, which God hath created to be received with thanksgiving of them which believe and know the truth. **For every creature of God is good, and nothing to be refused, if it be received with thanksgiving**: For it is sanctified by the word of God and prayer.

Romans 14:1-3, 5-9, 11-14, 21 Him that is **weak in the faith** receive ye, but not to doubtful disputations. For one believeth that he may eat all things: another, who is weak, eateth herbs. Let not him that eateth despise him that eateth not; and let not him which eateth not judge him that eateth: for God hath received him. **One man esteemeth one day above another: another esteemeth every day alike. Let every man be fully persuaded in his own mind. He that regardeth the day, regardeth it unto the Lord**; and he that regardeth not the day, to the Lord he doth not regard it. He that eateth, eateth to the Lord, for he giveth God thanks; and he that eateth not, to the Lord he eateth not, and giveth God thanks. For none of us liveth to himself, and no man dieth to himself. For whether we live, we live unto the Lord; and whether we die, we die unto the Lord: **whether we live therefore, or die, we are the Lord's**. For it is written, As I live, saith the Lord, **every knee shall bow** to me, and **every tongue shall confess** to God. So then **every one of us shall give account of himself to God**. Let us not therefore judge one another any more: but judge this rather, **that no man put a stumblingblock or an occasion to fall in his brother's way.** I know, and am persuaded by the Lord Jesus, that **there is nothing unclean of itself: but to him that esteemeth any thing to be unclean, to him it is unclean. It is good neither to eat flesh, nor to drink wine, nor any thing whereby thy brother stumbleth, is offended, or is made weak.**

107

Psalm 116:15 Precious in the sight of the Lord is the death of His saints.

Matthew 8:22 But Jesus said unto him, Follow Me; and let the dead bury their dead.

Proverbs 20:13 Do not love **sleep**, lest you come to poverty; Open your eyes, and you will be satisfied with bread.

Daniel 12:2 And many of those who **sleep** in the dust of the earth shall awake, Some to everlasting life, Some to shame and everlasting contempt.

Ephesians 5:14 Therefore He says: Awake, you who **sleep**, Arise from the dead, And Christ will give you light.

Job 14:12 So man lies down and does not rise. Till the Heavens are no more, They will not awake Nor be roused from their **sleep**.

1-Thessalonians 4:13-18 But I would not have you to be ignorant, brethren, concerning them which are asleep, that ye sorrow not, even as others which have no hope. For if we believe that Jesus died and rose again, even so them also which **sleep** in Jesus will God bring with Him. For this we say unto you by the word of the Lord, that we which are alive and remain unto the coming of the Lord shall not prevent them which are **asleep**. For the Lord Himself shall descend from Heaven with a shout, with the voice of the archAngel, and with the trump of God: and the dead in Christ shall rise first: Then we which are alive and remain shall be caught up together with them in the clouds, to meet the Lord in the air: and so shall we ever be with the Lord. Wherefore comfort one another with these words.

Mark 13:32 But of that day and that hour knowth no man, no, not the Angels which are in Heaven, neither the Son, but the Father.

Matthew 24:36 But of that day and hour knoweth no man, no, not the Angels of Heaven, but my Father only.

Luke 12:40 Be ye therefore ready also: for the Son of man cometh at an hour when ye think not.

2-Thessalonians 1:7-9 And to you who are troubled rest with us, **when the Lord Jesus shall be revealed from Heaven with his mighty angels, In flaming fire taking vengeance on them that know not God**, and that obey not the gospel of our Lord Jesus Christ: Who shall be punished with everlasting destruction from the presence of the Lord, and from the glory of his power;

Matthew 7:21-23 **Not every one that saith unto Me, Lord, Lord, shall enter into the kingdom of Heaven; but he that doeth the will of My Father which is in Heaven.** Many will say to Me in that day, Lord, Lord, have we not prophesied in thy name? and in thy name have cast out devils? and in thy name done many wonderful works? And then will I profess unto them, I never knew you: depart from Me, ye that work iniquity.

1-Thessalonians 5:1-8 But of the times and the seasons, brethren, ye have no need that I write unto you. For yourselves know perfectly that the **day of the Lord so cometh as a thief in the night**. For when they shall say, Peace and safety; then sudden destruction cometh upon them, as travail upon a woman with child; and they shall not escape. But ye, brethren, are not in darkness, that that day should overtake you as a thief. Ye are all the children of light, and the children of the day: we are not of the night, nor of darkness. Therefore **let us not sleep**, as others do, **but let us watch and be sober**. For they that sleep sleep in the night; and they that be drunken are drunken in the night. But let us, who are of the day, be sober, putting on the breastplate of faith and love; and for an helmet, the hope of salvation.

2-Timothy 4:7-8 I have fought a good fight, I have finished my course, I have kept the faith: Henceforth there is laid up for me a crown of righteousness, which the Lord, the righteous judge, shall give me at that day: and not to me only, but unto all them also that love his appearing.

Ephesians 4:30 And grieve not the Holy Spirit of God, whereby we are sealed unto the day of redemption.

Matthew 22:24-32 Saying, Master, Moses said, If a man die, having no children, his brother shall marry his wife, and raise up seed unto his brother. Now there were with us seven brethren: and the first, when he had married a wife, deceased, and, having no issue, left his wife unto his brother: Likewise the second also, and the third, unto the seventh. And last of all the woman died also. Therefore in the resurrection whose wife shall she be of the seven? for they all had her. Jesus answered and said unto them, Ye do err, not knowing the scriptures, nor the power of God. For in the resurrection they neither marry, nor are given in marriage, but are as the Angels of God in Heaven. But as touching the resurrection of the dead, have ye not read that which was spoken unto you by God, saying, I am the God of Abraham, and the God of Isaac, and the God of Jacob? God is not the God of the dead, but of the living.

2-Peter 3:8-9 With Him **a thousand years** is as one day. The Lord is longsuffering towards us, and He is not willing that any should perish, but that all should come to repentance.

Psalm 90:4 For **a thousand years** in Your sight are like yesterday when it is past, And like a watch in the night.

Ephesians 5:15-18 See then that ye walk circumspectly, not as fools, but as wise, **Redeeming the time**, because the days are evil. Wherefore be ye not unwise, but understanding what the will of the Lord is. And be not drunk with wine, but be filled with the Spirit.

Colossians 4:5 Walk in wisdom toward them that are without, **redeeming the time.**

Matthew 6:30, 31, 33-34 But **seek ye first the kingdom of God**, and His righteousness; and all these things shall be added to you. Take therefore no thought for the morrow: for the morrow shall take thought for the things of itself. Sufficient unto the day is the evil thereof.

Luke 12:31-32, 34 But rather **seek ye the kingdom of God**; and all these things shall be added unto you. Fear not, little flock; for it is your Father's good pleasure to give you the kingdom. For where your treasure is, there will your heart be also.

2-Timothy 2:15-16 Study to shew thyself approved unto God, a workman that needeth not to be ashamed, rightly dividing the word of truth. But shun profane and vain babblings: for they will increase unto more ungodliness.

Psalm 1:1-2 Blessed is the man that walketh not in the counsel of the ungodly, nor standeth in the way of sinners, nor sitteth in the seat of the scornful. But his delight is in the law of the Lord; and **in His law doth he meditate day and night.**

1-Peter 3:15 But sanctify the Lord God in your hearts: **and be ready always to give an answer** to every man that asketh you a reason of the hope that is in you with meekness and fear.

111

Matthew 13:1-17 The same day went Jesus out of the house, and sat by the sea side. And great multitudes were gathered together unto Him, so that He went into a ship, and sat; and the whole multitude stood on the shore. And **He spake many things unto them in parables**, saying, Behold, a sower went forth to sow; And when he sowed, some seeds fell by the way side, and the fowls came and devoured them up: Some fell upon stony places, where they had not much earth: and forthwith they sprung up, because they had no deepness of earth: And when the sun was up, they were scorched; and because they had no root, they withered away. And some fell among thorns; and the thorns sprung up, and choked them: But other fell into good ground, and brought forth fruit, some an hundredfold, some sixtyfold, some thirtyfold. Who hath ears to hear, let him hear. And the disciples came, and said unto Him, **Why speakest thou unto them in parables?** He answered and said unto them, Because it is given unto you to know the mysteries of the kingdom of Heaven, but to them it is not given. For whosoever hath, to him shall be given, and he shall have more abundance: but whosoever hath not, from him shall be taken away even that he hath. Therefore **speak I to them in parables: because they seeing see not; and hearing they hear not, neither do they understand.** And in them is fulfilled the prophecy of Esaias, which saith, By hearing ye shall hear, and shall not understand; and seeing ye shall see, and shall not perceive: For this people's heart is waxed gross, and their ears are dull of hearing, and their eyes they have closed; lest at any time they should see with their eyes and hear with their ears, and should understand with their heart, and should be converted, and I should heal them. But blessed are your eyes, for they see: and your ears, for they hear. For verily I say unto you, That many prophets and righteous men have desired to see those things which ye see, and have not seen them; and to hear those things which ye hear, and have not heard them.

Matthew 13:18-23 Hear ye therefore the **parable of the sower**. When any one heareth the word of the kingdom, and understandeth it not, then cometh the wicked one, and catcheth away that which was sown in his heart. This is he which received seed by the way side. But he that received the seed into stony places, the same is he that heareth the word, and anon with joy receiveth it; Yet hath he not root in himself, but dureth for a while: for when tribulation or persecution ariseth because of the word, by and by he is offended. He also that received seed among the thorns is he that heareth the word; and the care of this world, and the deceitfulness of riches, choke the word, and he becometh unfruitful. But he that received seed into the good ground is he that heareth the word, and understandeth it; which also beareth fruit, and bringeth forth, some an hundredfold, some sixty, some thirty.

Matthew 13:24-30 Another parable put he forth unto them, saying, **The kingdom of Heaven is likened unto a man which sowed good seed in his field**: But while men slept, his enemy came and sowed tares among the wheat, and went his way. But when the blade was sprung up, and brought forth fruit, then appeared the tares also. So the servants of the householder came and said unto him, Sir, didst not thou sow good seed in thy field? from whence then hath it tares? He said unto them, An enemy hath done this. The servants said unto him, Wilt thou then that we go and gather them up? But he said, Nay; lest while ye gather up the tares, ye root up also the wheat with them. Let both grow together until the harvest: and in the time of harvest I will say to the reapers, Gather ye together first the tares, and bind them in bundles to burn them: but gather the wheat into my barn.

Matthew 13:31-32 Another parable put He forth unto them, saying, **The kingdom of Heaven is like to a grain of mustard seed**, which a man took, and sowed in his field: Which indeed is the least of all seeds: but when it is grown, it is the greatest among herbs, and becometh a tree, so that the birds of the air come and lodge in the branches thereof.

Matthew 13:33 Another parable spake He unto them; **The kingdom of Heaven is like unto leaven**, which a woman took, and hid in three measures of meal, till the whole was leavened.

Matthew 13:34-35 All these things spake Jesus unto the multitude in parables; and **without a parable spake he not unto them**: That it might be fulfilled which was spoken by the prophet, saying, I will open my mouth in parables; I will utter things which have been kept secret from the foundation of the world.

Matthew 13:36-43 Then Jesus sent the multitude away, and went into the house: and His disciples came unto him, saying, **Declare unto us the parable of the tares of the field.** He answered and said unto them, He that soweth the good seed is the Son of man; The field is the world; the good seed are the children of the kingdom; but the tares are the children of the wicked one; The enemy that sowed them is the devil; the harvest is the end of the world; and the reapers are the angels. As therefore the tares are gathered and burned in the fire; so shall it be in the end of this world. The Son of man shall send forth his angels, and they shall gather out of His kingdom all things that offend, and them which do iniquity; And shall cast them into a furnace of fire: there shall be wailing and gnashing of teeth. Then shall the righteous shine forth as the sun in the kingdom of their Father. Who hath ears to hear, let him hear.

Matthew 13:44 Again, **the kingdom of Heaven is like unto treasure hid in a field**; the which when a man hath found, he hideth, and for joy thereof goeth and selleth all that he hath, and buyeth that field.

Matthew 13:45-46 Again, **the kingdom of Heaven is like unto a merchant man**, seeking goodly pearls: Who, when he had found one pearl of great price, went and sold all that he had, and bought it.

Matthew 13:47-50 Again, **the kingdom of Heaven is like unto a net**, that was cast into the sea, and gathered of every kind: Which, when it was full, they drew to shore, and sat down, and gathered the good into vessels, but cast the bad away. So shall it be at the end of the world: the angels shall come forth, and sever the wicked from among the just, And shall cast them into the furnace of fire: there shall be wailing and gnashing of teeth.

Matthew 22:2-14 The kingdom of Heaven is like unto a certain king, which made a marriage for his son, And sent forth his servants to call them that were bidden to the wedding: and they would not come. Again, he sent forth other servants, saying, Tell them which are bidden, Behold, I have prepared my dinner: my oxen and my fatlings are killed, and all things are ready: come unto the marriage. But they made light of it, and went their ways, one to his farm, another to his merchandise: And the remnant took his servants, and entreated them spitefully, and slew them. But when the king heard thereof, he was wroth: and he sent forth his armies, and destroyed those murderers, and burned up their city. Then saith he to his servants, The wedding is ready, but they which were bidden were not worthy. Go ye therefore into the highways, and as many as ye shall find, bid to the marriage. So those servants went out into the highways, and gathered together all as many as they found, both bad and good: and the wedding was furnished with guests. And when the king came in to see the guests, he saw there a man which had not on a wedding garment: And he saith unto him, Friend, how camest thou in hither not having a wedding garment? And he was speechless. Then said the king to the servants, Bind him hand and foot, and take him away, and cast him into outer darkness, there shall be weeping and gnashing of teeth. **For many are called, but few are chosen.**

Matthew 20:1-16 For the **kingdom of Heaven is like** a landowner who went out early in the morning to hire laborers for his vineyard. Now when he had agreed with the laborers for a denarius a day, he sent them into his vineyard. And he went out about the third hour and saw others standing idle in the marketplace, and said to them, You also go into the vineyard, and whatever is right I will give you. So they went. Again he went out about the sixth and the ninth hour, and did likewise. And about the eleventh hour

115

he went out and found others standing idle, and said to them, Why have you been standing here idle all day? They said to him, Because no one hired us. He said to them, You also go into the vineyard, and whatever is right you will receive. So when evening had come, the owner of the vineyard said to his steward, Call the laborers and give them their wages, beginning with the last to the first. And when those came who were hired about the eleventh hour, they each received a denarius. But when the first came, they supposed that they would receive more; and they likewise received each a denarius. And when they had received it, they complained against the landowner, saying, These last men have worked only one hour, and you made them equal to us who have borne the burden and the heat of the day. But he answered one of them and said, Friend, I am doing you no wrong. Did you not agree with me for a denarius? Take what is yours and go your way. I wish to give to this last man the same as to you. Is it not lawful for me to do what I wish with my own things? Or is your eye evil because I am good? **So the last shall be first, and the first last: for many be called, but few chosen.**

Matthew 18:1-6 At the same time came the disciples unto Jesus, saying, **Who is the greatest in the kingdom of Heaven?** And Jesus called a little child unto Him, and set him in the midst of them, And said, Verily I say unto you, **Except ye be converted, and become as little children, ye shall not enter into the kingdom of Heaven.** Whosoever therefore shall humble himself as this little child, the same is greatest in the **kingdom of Heaven**. And whoso shall receive one such little child in My name receiveth me. **But whoso shall offend one of these little ones which believe in Me, it were better for him that a millstone were hanged about his neck, and that he were drowned in the depth of the sea.**

Matthew 25:14-30 For **the kingdom of Heaven is** as a man travelling into a far country, who called his own servants, and delivered unto them his goods. And unto one he gave five talents, to another two, and to another one; to every man according to his several ability; and straightway took his journey. Then he that had received the five talents

116

went and traded with the same, and made them other five talents. And likewise he that had received two, he also gained other two. But he that had received one went and digged in the earth, and hid his Lord's money. After a long time the Lord of those servants cometh, and reckoneth with them. And so he that had received five talents came and brought other five talents, saying, Lord, thou deliveredst unto me five talents: behold, I have gained beside them five talents more. His Lord said unto him, Well done, thou good and faithful servant: thou hast been faithful over a few things, I will make thee ruler over many things: enter thou into the joy of thy Lord. He also that had received two talents came and said, Lord, thou deliveredst unto me two talents: behold, I have gained two other talents beside them. His Lord said unto him, **Well done, good and faithful servant; thou hast been faithful over a few things, I will make thee ruler over many things: enter thou into the joy of thy Lord.** Then he which had received the one talent came and said, Lord, I knew thee that thou art an hard man, reaping where thou hast not sown, and gathering where thou hast not strawed: And I was afraid, and went and hid thy talent in the earth: lo, there thou hast that is thine. His Lord answered and said unto him, Thou wicked and slothful servant, thou knewest that I reap where I sowed not, and gather where I have not strawed: Thou oughtest therefore to have put my money to the exchangers, and then at my coming I should have received mine own with usury. Take therefore the talent from him, and give it unto him which hath ten talents. For unto every one that hath shall be given, and he shall have abundance: but from him that hath not shall be taken away even that which he hath. And cast ye the unprofitable servant into outer darkness: there shall be weeping and gnashing of teeth.

Luke 18:15-17 And they brought unto Him also infants, that He would touch them: but when His disciples saw it, they rebuked them. But Jesus called them unto Him, and said, Suffer little children to come unto Me, and forbid them not: for of such is the **kingdom of God**. Verily I say unto you, Whosoever shall not receive the **kingdom of God** as a little child shall in no wise enter therein.

Luke 18:1-8 And He spake a parable unto them to this end, that men ought always to pray, and not to faint; saying There was in a city a judge, and there was a widow in that city; and she came to him saying, Avenge me of mine adversary. And he would not for a while: but afterward he said within himself, Yet because this widow troubleth me, I will avenge her, lest by her continual coming she weary me. And shall not God avenge His own elect, which cry day and night unto Him? I tell you that He will avenge them speedily.

Luke 21:29-36 And He spake to them a parable; Behold the fig tree, and all the trees; When they now shoot forth, ye see and know of your own selves that summer is now nigh at hand. So likewise ye, when ye see these things come to pass, know ye that the kingdom of God is nigh at hand. Verily I say unto you, This generation shall not pass away, till all be fulfilled. Heaven and earth shall pass away: but My words shall not pass away. And take heed to yourselves, lest at any time your hearts be overcharged with surfeiting, and drunkenness, and cares of this life, and so that day come upon you unawares. For as a snare shall it come on all them that dwell on the face of the whole earth. Watch ye therefore, and pray always, that ye may be accounted worthy to escape all these things that shall come to pass, and to stand before the Son of man.

Luke 17:20-21 And when He was demanded of the Pharisees, when the kingdom of God should come, He answered them and said, The kingdom of God cometh not with observation: Neither shall they say, Lo here! or, lo there! for, behold, **the kingdom of God is within you.**

Romans 14:17 For the **kingdom of God** is not meat and drink; but righteousness, and peace, and joy in the Holy Ghost.

Luke 15:11-14, 17-18, 20-22, 25, 28-32 (The Prodigal Son) A certain man had two sons: And the younger of them said to his Father, Father, give me the portion of goods that falleth to me. And not many days after the younger son gathered all together, and took his journey into a far country, and there wasted his substance with riotous living. And when he had spent all, there arose a mighty famine in that land; and he began to be in want. And when he came to himself, he said, How many hired servants of my Father's have bread enough and to spare, and I perish with hunger! I will arise and go to my Father and say: make me as one of thy hired servants. But when he was yet a great way off, his Father saw him, and had compassion, and ran, and fell on his neck, and kissed him. And the son said unto him, Father, I have sinned against Heaven, and in thy sight, and am no more worthy to be called thy son. But the Father said to his servants, Bring forth the best robe, and put it on him; and put a ring on his hand, and shoes on his feet: Now his elder son was in the field: and as he came and drew nigh to the house, he heard musick and dancing. And he was angry, and would not go in: therefore came his Father out, and intreated him. And he answering said to his Father, Lo, these many years do I serve thee, neither transgressed I at any time thy commandment: and yet thou never gavest me a kid, that I might make merry with my friends: But as soon as this thy son was come, which hath devoured thy living with harlots, thou hast killed for him the fatted calf. And he said unto him, **Son, thou art ever with me, and all that I have is thine.** We should be glad: for this thy brother was dead, and is alive again; and was lost, and is found.

1-Corinthians 6:9-11 Know ye not that the **unrighteous shall not inherit the kingdom of God**? Be not deceived: neither fornicators, nor idolaters, nor adulterers, nor effeminate, nor abusers of themselves with mankind, Nor thieves, nor covetous, nor drunkards, nor revilers, nor extortioners, shall inherit the kingdom of God. **And such were some of you: but ye are washed, but ye are sanctified, but ye are justified in the name of the Lord Jesus, and by the Spirit of our God.**

Ephesians 5:5 For this you know, that **no** fornicator, unclean person, nor covetous man, who is an idolater, **has any inheritance in the kingdom of Christ and God.**

Galatians 5:19-21 Now the works of the flesh are evident, which are: adultery, fornication, uncleanness, lewdness, idolatry, sorcery, hatred, contentions, jealousies, outbursts of wrath, selfish ambitions, dissensions, heresies, envy, murders, drunkenness, revelries, and the like; of which I tell you beforehand, just as I also told you in time past, that **those who practice such things will not inherit the kingdom of God**.

Matthew 5:20 That except your righteousness shall exceed the righteousness of the scribes and Pharisees, ye shall in no case enter into the kingdom of Heaven.

1-Corinthians 15:50 Now this I say, brethren, that **flesh and blood cannot inherit the kingdom of God**; neither doth corruption inherit incorruption.

1-Corinthians 3:16-17 **Know ye not that** ye are the temple of God, and that the Spirit of God dwelleth in you? If any man defile the temple of God, him shall God destroy; for the temple of God is holy, which temple ye are.

1-Corinthians 5:6 **Know ye not that** a little leaven leaveneth the whole lump?

1-Corinthians 6:2-3 Do **ye not know that** the saints shall judge the world? and if the world shall be judged by you, are ye unworthy to judge the smallest matters? **Know ye not that** we shall judge Angels? how much more things that pertain to this life?

1-Corinthians 6:15-16 **Know ye not that** your bodies are the members of Christ? shall I then take the members of Christ, and make them the members of an harlot? God forbid. What? **know ye not that** he which is joined to an harlot is one body?

1-Corinthians 6:19 What? **know ye not that** your body is the temple of the Holy Ghost which is in you, which ye have of God, and ye are not your own?

1-Corinthians 9:13 Do **ye not know that** they which minister about holy things live of the things of the temple? and they which wait at the altar are partakers with the altar?

1-Corinthians 9:24 **Know ye not that** they which run in a race run all, but one receiveth the prize? So run, that ye may obtain.

James 4:4 Ye adulterers and adulteresses, **know ye not that** the friendship of the world is enmity with God? whosoever therefore will be a friend of the world is the enemy of God.

Romans 6:3 **Know ye not, that** so many of us as were baptized into Jesus Christ were baptized into his death?

Romans 6:16 **Know ye not, that** to whom ye yield yourselves servants to obey, his servants ye are to whom ye obey; whether of sin unto death, or of obedience unto righteousness?

Romans 7:1 **Know ye not**, brethren, how **that** the law hath dominion over a man as long as he liveth?

Mark 4:13 And He said unto them, **Know ye not** this parable? and how then will ye know all parables?

Exodus 33:20-23   And He said, Thou canst not see My face: for **there shall no man see Me, and live.** And the LORD said, Behold, there is a place by Me, and thou shalt stand upon a rock: And it shall come to pass, while My glory passeth by, that I will put thee in a clift of the rock, and will cover thee with My hand while I pass by: And I will take away Mine hand, and thou shalt see My back parts: but **My face shall not be seen.**

Romans 8:1-5   There is therefore now no condemnation to them which are in Christ Jesus, who walk not after the flesh, but after **the Spirit**. For the law of the **Spirit of life** in Christ Jesus hath made me free from the law of sin and death. For what the law could not do, in that it was weak through the flesh, God sending his own Son in the likeness of sinful flesh, and for sin, condemned sin in the flesh: That the righteousness of the law might be fulfilled in us, who walk not after the flesh, but after **the Spirit**. For they that are after the flesh do mind the things of the flesh; but they that are after **the Spirit** the things of **the Spirit**.

Romans 8:6-11   For to be carnally minded is death; but to be spiritually minded is life and peace. Because the carnal mind is enmity against God: for it is not subject to the law of God, neither indeed can be. So then they that are in the flesh cannot please God. But ye are not in the flesh, but in **the Spirit**, if so be that the **Spirit of God** dwell in you. Now if any man have not the **Spirit of Christ**, he is none of His. And if Christ be in you, the body is dead because of sin; but **the Spirit** is life because of righteousness. But if the **Spirit of Him** that raised up Jesus from the dead dwell in you, He that raised up Christ from the dead shall also quicken your mortal bodies by **His Spirit** that dwelleth in you.

John 4:24   **God is a Spirit**: and they that worship Him must worship Him in **Spirit** and in truth.

123

Acts 4:31 And when they had prayed, the place was shaken where they were assembled together; **and they were all filled with the Holy Ghost,** and they spake the word of God with boldness.

Romans 8:26 Likewise the **Spirit** also helpeth our infirmities: for we know not what we should pray for as we ought: but the Spirit itself maketh intercession for us with groanings which cannot be uttered.

1-Thessalonians 5:19 Quench not **the Spirit**.

Matthew 3:11 I indeed baptize you with water unto repentence. But He that cometh after me is mightier than I, whose shoes I am not worthy to bear: He shall baptize you with **the Holy Ghost**, and with fire:

Galatians 6:7-8 Be not deceived; God is not mocked: for whatsoever a man soweth, that shall he also reap. For he that soweth to his flesh shall of the flesh reap corruption; but he that soweth to **the Spirit** shall of **the Spirit** reap life everlasting.

Ephesians 4:4-7 There is one body, and one **Spirit**, even as ye are called in one hope of your calling; One Lord, one faith, one baptism, One God and Father of all, who is above all, and through all, and in you all. But unto every one of us is given grace according to the measure of the gift of Christ.

Luke 23:46 And when Jesus had cried with a loud voice. He said. Father. into thy hands I commend my **Spirit**: and having said thus, **He gave up the ghost.**

John 14:1-2, 26 Let not your heart be troubled: ye believe in God, believe also in me. In My Father's house are many mansions: if it were not so, I would have told you. I go to prepare a place for you. But **the Comforter, which is the Holy Ghost, whom the Father will send in My name,** he shall teach you all things, and bring all things to your remembrance, whatsoever I have said unto you.

124

John 16:7 Nevertheless I tell you the truth; It is expedient for you that I go away: for if I go not away, **the Comforter** will not come unto you; but if I depart, I will send him unto you.

Luke 12:10 And whosoever shall speak a word against the Son of man, it shall be forgiven him: but unto him that **blasphemeth against the Holy Ghost** it shall not be forgiven.

Mark 3:28-29 Verily I say unto you, All sins shall be forgiven unto the sons of men, and blasphemies wherewith soever they shall blaspheme: But he that shall **blaspheme against the Holy Ghost** hath never forgiveness, but is in danger of eternal damnation.

Matthew 12:31-32 Wherefore I say unto you, All manner of sin and blasphemy shall be forgiven unto men: but the **blasphemy against the Holy Ghost** shall not be forgiven unto men. And whosoever speaketh a word against the Son of man, it shall be forgiven him: but whosoever **speaketh against the Holy Ghost**, it shall not be forgiven him, neither in this world, neither in the world to come.

John 7:39 But this spake He of **the Spirit**, which they that believe on Him should receive: **for the Holy Ghost was not yet given; because that Jesus was not yet glorified.**

1-Corinthians 12:8-10 (9 Spiritual Gifts) For to one is given by the Spirit the word of wisdom; to another the word of knowledge by the same Spirit; To another faith by the same Spirit; to another the gifts of healing by the same Spirit; To another the working of miracles; to another prophecy; to another discerning of spirits; to another divers kinds of tongues; to another the interpretation of tongues:

1-Corinthians 14:1-40 (Speaking in Tongue) **Follow after charity, and desire spiritual gifts, but rather that ye may prophesy. For he that speaketh in an unknown tongue speaketh not unto men, but unto God:** for no man understandeth him; howbeit in the spirit he speaketh mysteries. But he that prophesieth speaketh unto men to

125

edification, and exhortation, and comfort. **He that speaketh in an unknown tongue edifieth himself; but he that prophesieth edifieth the church.** I would that ye all spake with tongues but rather that ye prophesied: for greater is he that prophesieth than he that speaketh with tongues, except he interpret, that the church may receive edifying. Now, brethren, if I come unto you speaking with tongues, what shall I profit you, except I shall speak to you either by revelation, or by knowledge, or by prophesying, or by doctrine? And even things without life giving sound, whether pipe or harp, except they give a distinction in the sounds, how shall it be known what is piped or harped? For if the trumpet give an uncertain sound, who shall prepare himself to the battle? So likewise ye, except ye utter by the tongue words easy to be understood, how shall it be known what is spoken? for ye shall speak into the air. There are, it may be, so many kinds of voices in the world, and none of them is without signification. Therefore if I know not the meaning of the voice, I shall be unto him that speaketh a barbarian, and he that speaketh shall be a barbarian unto me. Even so ye, forasmuch as ye are zealous of spiritual gifts, seek that ye may excel to the edifying of the church. Wherefore let him that speaketh in an unknown tongue pray that he may interpret. For if I pray in an unknown tongue, my spirit prayeth, but my understanding is unfruitful. What is it then? I will pray with the spirit, and I will pray with the understanding also: I will sing with the spirit, and I will sing with the understanding also. Else when thou shalt bless with the spirit, how shall he that occupieth the room of the unlearned say Amen at thy giving of thanks, seeing he understandeth not what thou sayest? For thou verily givest thanks well, but the other is not edified. I thank my God, I speak with tongues more than ye all: **Yet in the church I had rather speak five words with my understanding, that by my voice I might teach others also, than ten thousand words in an unknown tongue.** Brethren, be not children in understanding: howbeit in malice be ye children, but in understanding be men. In the law it is written, With men of other tongues and other lips will I speak unto this people; and yet for all that will they not hear Me, saith the Lord. Wherefore tongues are for a sign, not to them that believe, but to them that believe not: but prophesying serveth not for them that believe not, but for them which believe. If therefore the whole church be come together into one place, and all speak with tongues, and there come in those that are unlearned, or unbelievers, will they not say that ye are mad? But if all prophesy, and there come in one that believeth not, or one unlearned, he is convinced of all, he is judged of all: And thus are the secrets of his heart made manifest; and so falling down on his face he will worship God, and report that God is in you of a truth. How is it then, brethren? when ye come together, every one of you hath a psalm, hath a doctrine, hath a tongue, hath a revelation, hath an interpretation. Let all things be done unto edifying. **If any man speak in an unknown tongue, let it be by two, or at the most by three, and that by course; and let one interpret. But if there be no interpreter, let him keep silence in the church; and let him speak to himself, and to God.** Let the prophets speak two or three, and let the other judge. If any thing be revealed to another that sitteth by, let the first hold his peace. For ye may all prophesy one by one, that all may learn, and all may be comforted. And the spirits of the prophets are subject to the prophets. For God is not the author of confusion, but of peace, as in all churches of the saints. **Let your women keep silence in the churches: for it is not permitted unto them to speak; but they are commanded to be under obedience as also saith the law. And if they will learn any thing, let them ask their husbands at home: for it is a shame for women to speak in the church.** What? came the word of God out from you? or came it unto you only? If any man think himself to be a prophet, or spiritual, let him acknowledge that the things that I write unto you are the commandments of the Lord. But if any man be ignorant, let him be ignorant. Wherefore, brethren, covet to prophesy, and forbid not to speak with tongues. **Let all things be done decently and in order.**

Matthew 26:47-56 And while He yet spake, lo, Judas, one of the twelve, came, and with him a great multitude with swords and staves, from the chief priests and elders of the people. Now he that betrayed Him gave them a sign, saying, Whomsoever I shall kiss, that same is He: hold Him fast. And forthwith he came to Jesus, and said, Hail, master; and kissed Him. And Jesus said unto him, Friend, wherefore art thou come? Then came they, and laid hands on Jesus and took Him. And, behold, one of them which were with Jesus stretched out his hand, and drew his sword, and struck a servant of the high priest's, and smote off his ear. Then said Jesus unto him, Put up again thy sword into his place: for all they that take the sword shall perish with the sword. Thinkest thou that I cannot now pray to my Father, and He shall presently give Me more than twelve legions of Angels? But how then shall the scriptures be fulfilled, that thus it must be? In that same hour said Jesus to the multitudes, Are ye come out as against a thief with swords and staves for to take Me? I sat daily with you teaching in the temple, and ye laid no hold on Me. **But all this was done, that the scriptures of the prophets might be fulfilled. Then all the disciples forsook Him, and fled.**

Matthew 26:69-75 Now Peter sat without in the palace: and a damsel came unto him, saying, Thou also wast with Jesus of Galilee. But he denied before them all, saying, I know not what thou sayest. And when he was gone out into the porch, another maid saw him, and said unto them that were there, This fellow was also with Jesus of Nazareth. And again he denied with an oath, I do not know the man. And after a while came unto him they that stood by, and said to Peter, Surely thou also art one of them; for thy speech betrayeth thee. Then began he to curse and to swear, saying, I know not the man. And immediately the cock crew. **And Peter remembered the word of Jesus, which said unto him, Before the cock crow, thou shalt deny Me thrice.** And he went out, and wept bitterly.

Matthew 27:1-10 When the morning was come, all the chief priests and elders of the people took counsel against Jesus to put Him to death: And when they had bound Him, they led Him away, and delivered Him to Pontius Pilate the governor. Then Judas, which had betrayed Him, when he saw that He was condemned, repented himself, and brought again the thirty pieces of silver to the chief priests and elders, Saying, I have sinned in that I have betrayed the innocent blood. And they said, What is that to us? see thou to that. And he cast down the pieces of silver in the temple, and departed, and went and hanged himself. And the chief priests took the silver pieces, and said, It is not lawful for to put them into the treasury, because it is the price of blood. And they took counsel, and bought with them the potter's field, to bury strangers in. Wherefore that field was called, The field of blood, unto this day. **Then was fulfilled that which was spoken by Jeremy the prophet,** saying, And they took the thirty pieces of silver, the price of Him that was valued, whom they of the children of Israel did value; And gave them for the potter's field, as the Lord appointed me.

Matthew 27:27-35 Then the soldiers of the governor took Jesus into the common hall, and gathered unto Him the whole band of soldiers. And they stripped Him, and put on Him a scarlet robe. And when they had platted a crown of thorns, they put it upon His head, and a reed in His right hand: and they bowed the knee before Him, and mocked Him, saying, Hail, King of the Jews! And they spit upon Him, and took the reed, and smote Him on the head. And after that they had mocked Him, they took the robe off from Him, and put His own raiment on Him, and led Him away to crucify Him. And as they came out, they found a man of Cyrene, Simon by name: him they compelled to bear His cross. And when they were come unto a place called Golgotha, that is to say, a place of a skull, They gave Him vinegar to drink mingled with gall: and when He had tasted thereof, He would not drink. And they crucified Him, and parted His garments, casting lots: **that it might be fulfilled which was spoken by the prophet**, They parted my garments among them, and upon my vesture did they cast lots.

Mark 14:43-49 And immediately, while He yet spake, cometh Judas, one of the twelve, and with him a great multitude with swords and staves, from the chief priests and the scribes and the elders. And he that betrayed Him had given them a token, saying, Whomsoever I shall kiss, that same is He; take Him, and lead Him away safely. And as soon as he was come, he goeth straightway to Him, and saith, Master, Master; and kissed Him. And they laid their hands on Him, and took Him. And one of them that stood by drew a sword, and smote a servant of the high priest, and cut off his ear. And Jesus answered and said unto them, Are ye come out, as against a thief, with swords and with staves to take me? I was daily with you in the temple teaching, and ye took me not: **but the scriptures must be fulfilled.**

Mark 14:66-72 And as Peter was beneath in the palace, there cometh one of the maids of the high priest: And when she saw Peter warming himself, she looked upon him, and said, And thou also wast with Jesus of Nazareth. But he denied, saying, I know not, neither understand I what thou sayest. And he went out into the porch; and the cock crew. And a maid saw him again, and began to say to them that stood by, This is one of them. And he denied it again. And a little after, they that stood by said again to Peter, Surely thou art one of them: for thou art a Galilaean, and thy speech agreeth thereto. But he began to curse and to swear, saying, I know not this man of whom ye speak. And the second time the cock crew. **And Peter called to mind the word that Jesus said unto him, Before the cock crow twice, thou shalt deny Me thrice.** And when he thought thereon, he wept.

Mark 15:25-28 And it was the third hour, and they crucified Him. And the superscription of his accusation was written over, THE KING OF THE JEWS. And with Him they crucify two thieves; the one on His right hand, and the other on His left. **And the scripture was fulfilled,** which saith, And He was numbered with the transgressors.

Matthew 8:17 **That it might be fulfilled which was spoken by Esaias the prophet**, saying, Himself took our infirmities, and bare our sicknesses.

130

Matthew 13:14 And in them is fulfilled the prophecy of **Esaias,** which saith, By hearing ye shall hear, and shall not understand, and seeing ye shall see, and shall not perceive.

Matthew 1:18-25 Now the birth of Jesus Christ was on this wise: When as his mother Mary was espoused to Joseph, before they came together, she was found with child of the Holy Ghost. Then Joseph her husband, being a just man, and not willing to make her a public example, was minded to put her away privily. But while he thought on these things, behold, the angel of the LORD appeared unto him in a dream, saying, Joseph, thou son of David, fear not to take unto thee Mary thy wife: for that which is conceived in her is of the Holy Ghost. And she shall bring forth a son, and thou shalt call His name JESUS: for He shall save his people from their sins. **Now all this was done, that it might be fulfilled which was spoken of the Lord by the prophet, saying,** Behold, a virgin shall be with child, and shall bring forth a son, and they shall call His name Emmanuel, which being interpreted is, God with us. Then Joseph being raised from sleep did as the angel of the Lord had bidden him, and took unto him his wife: And knew her not till she had brought forth her firstborn son: and he called His name JESUS.

Matthew 13:34-35 All these things spake Jesus unto the multitude in parables; and without a parable spake He not unto them: **That it might be fulfilled which was spoken by the prophet,** saying, I will open my mouth in parables; I will utter things which have been kept secret from the foundation of the world.

Luke 24:44 And He said unto them, These are the words which I spake unto you, while I was yet with you, **that all things must be fulfilled, which were written in the law of Moses, and in the prophets, and in the psalms, concerning Me.**

John 13:18 I speak not of you all: I know whom I have chosen: but **that the scripture may be fulfilled,** he that eateth bread with Me hath lifted up his heel against Me.

John 12:37-41 But though He had done so many miracles before them, yet they believed not on Him: **That the saying of Esaias the prophet might be fulfilled,** which he spake, Lord, who hath believed our report? and to whom hath the arm of the Lord been revealed? Therefore they could not believe, because that Esaias said again, He hath blinded their eyes, and hardened their heart; that they should not see with their eyes, nor understand with their heart, and be converted, and I should heal them. These things said Esaias, when he saw His glory, and spake of Him.

1-Corinthians 11:4, 7-9, 14-15 Every man praying or prophesying, having his head covered, dishonoureth his head. **For a man indeed ought not to cover his head, forasmuch as he is the image and glory of God**: but the woman is the glory of the man. For the man is not of the woman; but the woman of the man. **Neither was the man created for the woman; but the woman for the man.** Does not even nature itself teach you that if a man has long hair, it is a dishonor to him? But if a woman has long hair, it is a glory to her; for her hair is given to her for a covering.

Psalm 139:14 I will praise thee; for **I am fearfully and wonderfully made:** marvelous are thy works; and that my soul knoweth right well.

Romans 14:8 For whether we live, we live unto the Lord; and whether we die, we die unto the Lord: **whether we live therefore, or die, we are the Lord's.**

Genesis 6:1-3 And it came to pass, when men began to multiply on the face of the earth, and daughters were born unto them, That the sons of God saw the daughters of men that they were fair; and they took them wives of all which they chose. And the LORD said, My spirit shall not always strive with man, for that he also is flesh: yet his days shall be an **hundred and twenty years**.

Psalm 90:10 The days of our lives are **seventy years**; And if by reason of strength they are eighty years, Yet their boast is only labor and sorrow; For it is soon cut off, and we fly away.

Ecclesiastes 11:8-9 But if a man live many years, and rejoice in them all; **yet let him remember the days of darkness; for they shall be many.** Let thy heart cheer thee in the days of thy youth, and walk in the ways of thine heart, and in the sight of thine eyes: but know thou, **that for all these things God will bring thee into judgment.**

133

Jeremiah 9:23-24 Thus saith the LORD, Let not the wise man glory in his wisdom, neither let the mighty man glory in his might, let not the rich man glory in his riches: But **let him that glorieth glory** in this, **that he understandeth and knoweth Me, that I am the** LORD **which exercise lovingkindness, judgment, and righteousness, in the earth: for in these things I delight, saith the** LORD.

Psalm 23:1-6 **The** LORD **is my shepherd; I shall not want.** He maketh me to lie down in green pastures: He leadeth me beside the still waters. He restoreth my soul: He leadeth me in the paths of righteousness for His name's sake. Yea, though I walk through the valley of the shadow of death, I will fear no evil: for Thou art with me; thy rod and thy staff they comfort me. Thou preparest a table before me in the presence of Mine enemies: Thou anointest my head with oil; my cup runneth over. Surely goodness and mercy shall follow me all the days of my life: and I will dwell in the house of the LORD for ever.

1-Corinthians 7:23-24 **Ye are bought with a price;** be not ye the servants of men. Brethren, let every man, wherein he is called, therein abide with God.

Luke 12:6-7 Are not five sparrows sold for two farthings, and not one of them is forgotten before God? **But even the very hairs of your head are all numbered.** Fear not therefore: ye are of more value than many sparrows.

Romans 8:35-39 Who shall separate us from the love of Christ? shall tribulation, or distress, or persecution, or famine, or nakedness, or peril, or sword? As it is written, For thy sake we are killed all the day long; we are accounted as sheep for the slaughter. Nay, in all these things **we are more than conquerors through Him that loved us. For I am persuaded, that neither death, nor life, nor angels, nor principalities, nor powers, nor things present, nor things to come, Nor height, nor depth, nor any other creature, shall be able to separate us from the love of God, which is in Christ Jesus our Lord.**

1-Corinthians 6:13 Now the body is not for fornication, but for the Lord; and the Lord for the body.

Genesis 4:1-2, 8, 15-19, 25-26 And Adam knew Eve his wife; and she conceived, and bare Cain, and said, I have gotten a man from the LORD. And she again bare his brother Abel. And Cain talked with Abel his brother: and it came to pass, when they were in the field, that Cain rose up against Abel his brother, and slew him. And the LORD said unto him, Therefore whosoever slayeth Cain, vengeance shall be taken on him sevenfold. And the LORD set a mark upon Cain, **lest any finding him** should kill him. And Cain went out from the presence of the LORD, and **dwelt in the land of Nod**, on the east of Eden. **And Cain knew his wife**; and she conceived, and bare Enoch: And unto Enoch was born Irad: and Irad begat Mehujael: and Mehujael begat Methusael: and Methusael begat Lamech. And Lamech took unto him two wives: the name of the one was Adah, and the name of the other Zillah. And Adam knew his wife again; and she bare a son, and called his name Seth: For God, said she, hath appointed me another seed instead of Abel, whom Cain slew. And to Seth, to him also there was born a son; and he called his name Enos: then began men to call upon the name of the LORD. **(Note that God made Adam and Eve *first*, but He also made other people elsewhere *second*; we are not descendants of incest.)**

Psalm 100:3 Know ye that the Lord He is God: it is He that hath made us, and not we ourselves; we are His people, and the sheep of His pasture.

Psalm 27:1,4 The Lord is my light and my salvation; whom shall I fear? the Lord is the strength of my life; of whom shall I be afraid? One thing have I desired of the Lord, that will I seek after; that I may dwell in the house of the Lord all the days of my life, to behold the beauty of the Lord, and to enquire in His temple.

Ecclesiastes 9:11 I returned and saw under the sun that The race is not to the swift, Nor the battle to the strong, Nor bread to the wise, Nor riches to men of understanding, Nor **favor** to men of skill; But time, chance happen to them all.

Proverbs 31:10-31 **Who can find a virtuous woman?** for her price is far above rubies. The heart of her husband doth safely trust in her, so that he shall have no need of spoil. She will do him good and not evil all the days of her life. She seeketh wool, and flax, and worketh willingly with her hands. She is like the merchants' ships; she bringeth her food from afar. She riseth also while it is yet night, and giveth meat to her household, and a portion to her maidens. She considereth a field, and buyeth it: with the fruit of her hands she planteth a vineyard. She girdeth her loins with strength, and strengtheneth her arms. She perceiveth that her merchandise is good: her candle goeth not out by night. She layeth her hands to the spindle, and her hands hold the distaff. She stretcheth out her hand to the poor; yea, she reacheth forth her hands to the needy. She is not afraid of the snow for her household: for all her household are clothed with scarlet. She maketh herself coverings of tapestry; her clothing is silk and purple. Her husband is known in the gates, when he sitteth among the elders of the land. She maketh fine linen, and selleth it; and delivereth girdles unto the merchant. Strength and honour are her clothing; and she shall rejoice in time to come. She openeth her mouth with wisdom; and in her tongue is the law of kindness. She looketh well to the ways of her household, and eateth not the bread of idleness. Her children arise up, and call her blessed; her husband also, and he praiseth her. Many daughters have done virtuously, but thou excellest them all. Favour is deceitful, and beauty is vain: but a woman that feareth the LORD, she shall be praised. Give her of the fruit of her hands; and let her own works praise her in the gates.

Jeremiah 17:8 For he shall be like a tree planted by the waters, Which spreads out its roots by the river, And will not fear when heat comes; But its leaf will be green, And will not be anxious in the year of drought, Nor will cease from yielding fruit.

Psalm 1:3 He shall be like a tree planted by the rivers of water, That brings forth its fruit in its season, Whose leaf also shall not wither; And whatever he does shall prosper.

1-Corinthians 7:1-3 (to avoid fornication, get your own spouse) Now concerning the things whereof ye wrote unto me: It is good for a man not to touch a woman. Nevertheless, to avoid fornication, let every man have his own wife, and let every woman have her own husband. Let the husband render unto the wife due benevolence: and likewise also the wife unto the husband.

1-Corinthians 7:7-9 (unmarried/widows:better to marry than burn) For I would that all men were even as I myself. But every man hath his proper gift of God, one after this manner, and another after that. I say therefore to the unmarried and widows, it is good for them if they abide even as I. But if they cannot contain, let them marry: for it is better to marry than to burn.

1-Corinthians 7:10-12 (married: depart not, or then stay unmarried) And unto the married I command, yet not I, but the Lord, Let not the wife depart from her husband: But and if she depart, let her remain unmarried or be reconciled to her husband: and let not the husband put away his wife. But to the rest speak I, not the Lord: If any brother hath a wife that believeth not, and she be pleased to dwell with him, let him not put her away.

1-Corinthians 7:13-16 (a married may save the unbelieving spouse) And the woman which hath an husband that believeth not, and if he be pleased to dwell with her, let her not leave him. For the unbelieving husband is sanctified by the wife, and the unbelieving wife is sanctified by the husband: else were your children unclean; but now are they holy. But if the unbelieving depart, let him depart. A brother or a sister is not under bondage in such cases: but God hath called us to peace. **For what knowest thou, O wife, whether thou shalt save thy husband? or how knowest thou, O man, whether thou shalt save thy wife?**

1-Corinthians 7:25-31 (virgins:expect trouble in the flesh) Now concerning virgins I have no commandment of the Lord: yet I give my judgment, as one that hath obtained mercy of the Lord to be faithful. I suppose therefore that this is good for the present distress, I say, that it is good for a man so to be. **Art thou bound unto a wife? seek not to be loosed. Art thou loosed from a wife? seek not a wife.** But and if thou marry, thou hast not sinned; and if a virgin marry, she hath not sinned. Nevertheless such shall have trouble in the flesh: but I spare you. But this I say, brethren, the time is short: it remaineth, that both they that have wives be as though they had none; And they that weep, as though they wept not; and they that rejoice, as though they rejoiced not; and they that buy, as though they possessed not; And they that use this world, as not abusing it: for the fashion of this world passeth away.

1-Corinthians 7:32-34 (unmarried cares for Lord; married for world)   But I would have you without carefulness. He that is unmarried careth for the things that belong to the Lord, how he may please the Lord: But he that is married careth for the things that are of the world, how he may please his wife.   There is difference also between a wife and a virgin. The unmarried woman careth for the things of the Lord, that she may be holy both in body and in spirit: but she that is married careth for the things of the world, how she may please her husband.

1-Corinthians 7:36-38 (marriage is good but non-marriage is better) But if any man think that he behaveth himself uncomely toward his virgin, if she pass the flower of her age, and need so require, let him do what he will, he sinneth not: let them marry. Nevertheless he that standeth stedfast in his heart, having no necessity, but hath power over his own will, and hath so decreed in his heart that he will keep his virgin, doeth well. So then he that giveth her in marriage doeth well; but he that giveth her not in marriage doeth better.

1-Corinthians 7:39-40 (marriage bound by law as long as spouse lives) The wife is bound by the law as long as her husband liveth; but if her husband be dead, she is at liberty to be married to whom she will; only in the Lord. But she is happier if she so abide, after my judgment: and I think also that I have the Spirit of God.

Ephesians 5:22-31 **Wives, submit yourselves unto your own husbands,** as unto the Lord. For the husband is the head of the wife. Therefore, as the church is subject unto Christ, so let the wives be to their husbands in every thing. **Husbands, love your wives,** even as Christ also loved the church, and gave Himself for it. That He might sanctify and cleanse it with the washing of water by the word, That he might present it to Himself a glorious church, not having spot, or wrinkle, or any such thing; but that it should be holy and without blemish. **So ought men to love their wives as their own bodies. He that loveth his wife loveth himself.** For no man ever yet hated his own flesh; but nourisheth and cherisheth it, even as the Lord the church: For we are members of His body, of His flesh, and of His bones. **For this cause shall a man leave his father and mother, and shall be joined unto his wife, and they two shall be one flesh.** This is a great mystery: but I speak concerning Christ and the church. Nevertheless **let every one of you in particular so love his wife even as himself; and the wife see that she reverence her husband.**

Colossians 3:18-19 **Wives, submit yourselves unto your own husbands**, as it is fit in the Lord. **Husbands, love your wives,** and be not bitter against them.

1-Corinthians 7:4-6 **The wife hath not power of her own body, but the husband: and likewise also the husband hath not power of his own body, but the wife. Defraud ye not one the other, except it be with consent for a time, that ye may give yourselves to fasting and prayer; and come together again, that Satan tempt you not for your incontinency.** But I speak this by permission, and not of commandment.

Genesis 3:16 Unto the woman He said, I will greatly multiply thy sorrow and thy conception; in sorrow thou shalt bring forth children; and **thy desire shall be to thy husband, and he shall rule over thee.**

1-Corinthians 11:3 But I would have you know, that the **head of every man is Christ; and the head of the woman is the man;** and the **head of Christ is God.**

Ecclesiastes 2:24 **A man can do nothing better** than to eat and drink and find satisfaction in his work.

Ecclesiastes 3:22 So I saw that there is **nothing better for a man** than to enjoy his work, because that is his lot.

Ecclesiastes 8:15 So I commend the enjoyment of life, because **nothing is better for a man** under the sun than to eat and drink and be glad.

Ecclesiastes 9:9 **Enjoy life with your wife**, whom you love, all the days of this meaningless life that God has given you under the sun.

Proverbs 23:13-14 **Withhold not correction** from the child: for if thou beatest him with the rod, he shall not die. **Thou shalt beat him with the rod, and shalt deliver his soul from hell.**

Proverbs 22:6, 15 **Train up a child in the way he should go:** and when he is old, he will not depart from it. Foolishness is bound in the heart of a child; but **the rod of correction** shall drive it far from him.

Ecclesiastes 12:1 **Remember now thy Creator in the days of thy youth,** while the evil days come not, nor the years draw nigh, when thou shalt say, I have no pleasure in them;

Colossians 3:20 **Children**, obey your parents in all things: for this is well pleasing unto the Lord.

Ephesians 6:1-4 **Children,** obey your parents in the Lord: for this is right. **Honour thy father and mother; which is the first commandment with promise;** That it may be well with thee, and thou mayest live long on the earth. And, ye fathers, provoke not your children to wrath: but bring them up in the nurture and admonition of the Lord.

Proverbs 20:7 The just man walketh in his integrity: his children are blessed after him.

Matthew 15:4 For God commanded, saying Honour thy father and mother: and, **he that curseth father or mother, let him die the death.**

Proverbs 20:20 **Whoso curseth his father or his mother,** his lamp shall be put out in obscure darkness.

Luke 16:18 Whosoever putteth away his wife, and marrieth another, committeth adultery: and whosoever marrieth her that is put away from her husband committeth adultery.

Mark 10:2-12 And the Pharisees came to Him, and asked Him, **Is it lawful for a man to put away his wife?** tempting Him. And He answered and said unto them, What did Moses command you? And they said, Moses suffered to write a bill of divorcement, and to put her away. And Jesus answered and said unto them, **For the hardness of your heart he wrote you this precept. But from the beginning of the creation God made them male and female. For this cause shall a man leave his father and mother, and cleave to his wife;** And they twain shall be one flesh: so then they are no more twain, but one flesh. What therefore God hath joined together, let not man put asunder. And in the house His disciples asked Him again of the same matter. And He saith unto them, **Whosoever shall put away his wife, and marry another, committeth adultery against her. And if a woman shall put away her husband, and be married to another, she committeth adultery.**

Matthew 19:8-9 **From the beginning of time, it has never been okay to put away a wife, except it be for fornication.** And whosoever should put away his wife, except it be for fornication, and shall marry another, committeth adultery: and whoso marrieth her which is put away doth commit adultery.

Proverbs 21:9 and Proverbs 25:24 **It is better to dwell in a corner of the housetop,** than with a brawling woman in a wide house.

Proverbs 21:19 **It is better to dwell in the wilderness,** than with a contentious and angry woman.

1-Thessalonians 4:1-7 Furthermore then we beseech you, brethren, and exhort you by the Lord Jesus, that as ye have received of us how ye ought to walk and to please God, so ye would abound more and more. For ye know what commandments we gave you by the Lord Jesus. For this is the will of God, even your sanctification, that ye should **abstain from fornication:** That every one of you should know how to possess his vessel in sanctification and honour; Not in the lust of concupiscence, even as the Gentiles which know not God: That no man go beyond and defraud his brother in any matter: because that the Lord is the avenger of all such, as we also have forewarned you and testified. For God hath not called us unto uncleanness, but unto holiness.

1-Corinthians 6:18-20 Flee fornication. Every sin that a man doeth is without the body; but he that committeth fornication sinneth against his own body. What? know ye not that your body is the temple of the Holy Ghost which is in you, which ye have of God, and ye are not your own? For ye are bought with a price: therefore glorify God in your body, and in your spirit, which are God's.

Ephesians 5:3-4 But fornication, and all uncleanness, or covetousness, let it not be once named among you, as becometh saints; **Neither filthiness, nor foolish talking, nor jesting,** which are not convenient: **but rather giving of thanks.**

Proverbs 6:20-32 My son, keep thy father's commandment, and forsake not the law of thy mother: Bind them continually upon thine heart, and tie them about thy neck. When thou goest, it shall lead thee; when thou sleepest, it shall keep thee; and when thou awakest, it shall talk with thee. For the commandment is a lamp; and the law is light; and reproofs of instruction are the way of life: **To keep thee from the evil woman, from the flattery of**

143

the tongue of a strange woman. Lust not after her beauty in thine heart; neither let her take thee with her eyelids. **For by means of a whorish woman a man is brought to a piece of bread:** and the adultress will hunt for the precious life. **Can a man take fire in his bosom, and his clothes not be burned? Can one go upon hot coals, and his feet not be burned?** So he that goeth in to his neighbour's wife; whosoever toucheth her shall not be innocent. Men do not despise a thief, if he steal to satisfy his soul when he is hungry; But if he be found, he shall restore sevenfold; he shall give all the substance of his house. **But whoso committeth adultery with a woman lacketh understanding: he that doeth it destroyeth his own soul.**

<u>Proverbs 7:1-27</u> My son, keep my words, and lay up my commandments with thee. **Keep my commandments, and live;** and my law as the apple of thine eye. Bind them upon thy fingers, write them upon the table of thine heart. Say unto wisdom, Thou art my sister; and call understanding thy kinswoman: **That they may keep thee from the strange woman, from the stranger which flattereth with her words.** For at the window of my house I looked through my casement, And beheld among the simple ones, I discerned among the youths, a young man void of understanding, Passing through the street near her corner; and he went the way to her house, In the twilight, in the evening, in the black and dark night: And, behold, there met him **a woman with the attire of an harlot,** and subtil of heart. (She is loud and stubborn; her feet abide not in her house: Now is she without, **now in the streets, and lieth in wait at every corner.**) So she caught him, and kissed him, and with an impudent face said unto him, I have peace offerings with me; this day have I payed my vows. Therefore came I forth to meet thee, diligently to seek thy face, and I have found thee. I have decked my bed with coverings of tapestry, with carved works, with fine linen of Egypt. I have perfumed my bed with myrrh, aloes, and cinnamon. Come, let us take our fill of love until the morning: let us solace ourselves with loves. For the goodman is not at home, he is gone a long journey: He hath taken a bag of money with him, and will come home at the day appointed. With her much fair speech she caused him

to yield, with the flattering of her lips she forced him. He goeth after her straightway, as an ox goeth to the slaughter, or as a fool to the correction of the stocks; Till a dart strike through his liver; as a bird hasteth to the snare, and knoweth not that it is for his life. Hearken unto me now therefore, O ye children, and attend to the words of my mouth. Let not thine heart decline to her ways, go not astray in her paths. For she hath cast down many wounded: yea, **many strong men have been slain by her. Her house is the way to hell, going down to the chambers of death.**

Genesis 19:30-38 And Lot went up out of Zoar, and dwelt in the mountain, and his two daughters with him; for he feared to dwell in Zoar: and he dwelt in a cave, he and his two daughters. And the firstborn said unto the younger, Our father is old, and there is not a man in the earth to come in unto us after the manner of all the earth: Come, let us make our father drink wine, and we will lie with him, that we may preserve seed of our father. And they made their father drink wine that night: and the firstborn went in, and lay with her father; and he perceived not when she lay down, nor when she arose. And it came to pass on the morrow, that the firstborn said unto the younger, Behold, I lay yesternight with my father: let us make him drink wine this night also; and go thou in, and lie with him, that we may preserve seed of our father. And they made their father drink wine that night also: and the younger arose, and lay with him; and he perceived not when she lay down, nor when she arose. **Thus were both the daughters of Lot with child by their father.** And the first born bare a son, and called his name Moab: the same is the father of the Moabites unto this day. And the younger, she also bare a son, and called his name Benammi: the same is the father of the children of Ammon unto this day.

Genesis 34:1-2, 7, 13-16, 24-29 And Dinah the daughter of Leah, which she bare unto Jacob, went out to see the daughters of the land. And when Shechem the son of Hamor the Hivite, prince of the country, saw her, he took her, and lay with her, and defiled her. And the sons of Jacob came out of the field when they heard it: and the men were grieved, and they were very wroth, because he had wrought folly in Israel in lying with Jacob's daughter: which thing ought not to be done. And the sons of Jacob answered Shechem and Hamor his father deceitfully, and said, because he had defiled Dinah their sister: And they said unto them, We cannot do this thing, to give our sister to one that is uncircumcised; for that were a reproach unto us: But in this will we consent unto you: If ye will be as we be, that every male of you be circumcised; Then will we give our daughters unto you, and we will take your daughters to us, and we will dwell with you, and we will become one people. And unto Hamor and unto Shechem his son hearkened all that went out of the gate of his city; **and every male was circumcised,** all that went out of the gate of his city. **And it came to pass on the third day, when they were sore, that two of the sons of Jacob, Simeon and Levi, Dinah's brethren, took each man his sword, and came upon the city boldly, and slew all the males.** And they slew Hamor and Shechem his son with the edge of the sword, and took Dinah out of Shechem's house, and went out. The sons of Jacob came upon the slain, and spoiled the city, because they had defiled their sister. They took their sheep, and their oxen, and their asses, and that which was in the city, and that which was in the field, And all their wealth, and all their little ones, and their wives took they captive, and spoiled even all that was in the house.

1-Corinthians 10:8 Neither let us commit fornication, as some of them committed, and fell in one day three and twenty thousand.

1-Timothy 3:1-13 This is a true saying, if a man desire the office of a bishop, he desireth a good work. **A bishop** then **must be** blameless, **the husband of one wife**, vigilant, sober, of good behaviour, given to hospitality, apt to teach; Not given to wine, no striker, not greedy of filthy lucre; but patient, not a brawler, not covetous; One that ruleth well his own house, having his children in subjection with all gravity; (For if a man know not how to rule his own house, how shall he take care of the church of God?) Not a novice, lest being lifted up with pride he fall into the condemnation of the devil. Moreover he must have a good report of them which are without; lest he fall into reproach and the snare of the devil. **Likewise must the deacons be** grave, not doubletongued, not given to much wine, not greedy of filthy lucre; Holding the mystery of the faith in a pure conscience. And let these also first be proved; then let them use the office of a deacon, being found blameless. Even so must their wives be grave, not slanderers, sober, faithful in all things. **Let the deacons be the husbands of one wife, ruling their children and their own houses well.** For they that have used the office of a deacon well purchase to themselves a good degree, and great boldness in the faith which is in Christ Jesus.

Titus 1:5-9 Ordain **elders** in every city, as I had appointed thee: If any be blameless, the **husband of one wife**, having faithful children not accused of riot or unruly. For a **bishop** must be blameless, as the steward of God; not selfwilled, not soon angry, not given to wine, no striker, not given to filthy lucre; But a lover of hospitality, a lover of good men, sober, just, holy, temperate; Holding fast the faithful word as he hath been taught, that he may be able by sound doctrine both to exhort and to convince the gainsayers.

2-Timothy 4:2-3 Preach the word; be instant in season, out of season; reprove, rebuke, exhort with all long suffering and doctrine.

147

2-Timothy 3:16 All scripture is given by inspiration of God, and is profitable for doctrine, for reproof, for correction, for instruction in righteousness:

Mark 3:13-19 And He ordained 12 to send forth to preach; And to have power to heal sicknesses; And to cast out devils: Simon He surnamed Peter, Andrew, James the son of Zebedee, John the brother of James, Philip, Bertholomew, Matthew, Thomas, James the son of alphaeus, Simon the Canaanite, Thaddaeus, and Judas Iscariot.

Mark 16:15-16 And He said unto them, **Go ye into all the world, and preach the gospel to every creature. He that believeth and is baptized shall be saved; but he that believeth not shall be damned.**

Matthew 28:16-20 Then the eleven disciples went away into Galilee, into a mountain where Jesus had appointed them. And when they saw Him, they worshipped Him: but some doubted. And Jesus came and spake unto them, saying, All power is given unto Me in Heaven and in earth. Go ye therefore, and teach all nations, baptizing them in the name of the Father, and of the Son, and of the Holy Ghost: Teaching them to observe all things whatsoever I have commanded you: and, lo, I am with you always, even unto the end of the world. Amen.

Matthew 13:54-58 And when He was come into His own country, He taught them in their synagogue, insomuch that they were astonished, and said, Whence hath this man this wisdom, and these mighty works? Is not this the carpenter's son? is not his mother called Mary? and his brethren, James, and Joses, and Simon, and Judas? And his sisters, are they not all with us? Whence then hath this man all these things? And they were offended in Him. But Jesus said unto them, A prophet is not without honour, save in his own country, and in his own house. And He did not many mighty works there because of their unbelief.

148

Luke 14:26-33 If any man come to Me, and hate not his father, and mother, and wife, and children, and brethren, and sisters, yea, and his own life also, he cannot be My disciple. And whosoever doth not bear his cross, and come after Me, cannot be My disciple. **For which of you, intending to build a tower, sitteth not down first, and counteth the cost, whether he have sufficient to finish it?** Lest haply, after he hath laid the foundation, and is not able to finish it, all that behold it begin to mock him, Saying, This man began to build, and was not able to finish. Or what king, going to make war against another king, sitteth not down first, and consulteth whether he be able with ten thousand to meet him that cometh against him with twenty thousand? Or else, while the other is yet a great way off, he sendeth an ambassage, and desireth conditions of peace. **So likewise, whosoever he be of you that forsaketh not all that he hath, he cannot be My disciple.**

Hebrews 13:7,17,24 Remember, **obey, salute them that have the rule over you, and submit yourselves: for they watch for your souls, as they that must give account,** that they may do it with joy, and not with grief: for that is unprofitable for you.

1-Peter 2:13-18 **Submit yourselves to every ordinance of man for the Lord's sake:** whether it be to the king, as supreme; Or unto governors, as unto them that are sent by him for the punishment of evildoers, and for the praise of them that do well. For so is the will of God, that with well doing ye may put to silence the ignorance of foolish men: As free, and not using your liberty for a cloke of maliciousness, but as the servants of God. Honour all men. Love the brotherhood. Fear God. Honour the king. Servants, be subject to your masters with all fear; not only to the good and gentle, but also to the froward.

Hebrews 10:26 But if I **sin willfully** after I have received the knowledge of the truth, there remaineth no more sacrifice for sins.

Ecclesiastes 8:11 Because sentence against an **evil work is not executed speedily**, therefore the heart of the sons of men is fully set in them to do evil.

Luke 12:47-48 And that servant, which knew his Lord's will, and prepared not himself, neither did according to his will, shall be beaten with **many stripes**. But he that knew not, and did commit things worthy of stripes, shall be beaten with **few stripes**. For unto whomsoever much is given, of him shall be much required: and to whom men have committed much, of him they will ask the more.

Consequences Of Water From The Rock: Denied From Entering The Promised Land

Numbers 20:1-12 (**Exodus 17:1-7** is similar) Then came the children of Israel, even the whole congregation, into the desert of Zin in the first month: and the people abode in Kadesh; and Miriam died there, and was buried there. And there was no water for the congregation: and they gathered themselves together against Moses and against Aaron. And the people chode with Moses, and spake, saying, Would God that we had died when our brethren died before the LORD! And why have ye brought up the congregation of the LORD into this wilderness, that we and our cattle should die there? And wherefore have ye made us to come up out of Egypt, to bring us in unto this evil place? it is no place of seed, or of figs, or of vines, or of pomegranates; neither is there any water to drink. And Moses and Aaron went from the presence of the assembly unto the door of the tabernacle of the congregation, and they fell upon their faces: and the glory of the LORD appeared unto them. And the LORD spake unto Moses, saying, Take the rod, and gather thou the assembly together, thou, and Aaron thy brother, and speak ye unto the rock before their eyes; and it shall give forth his water, and thou shalt bring forth to them water out of the rock: so thou shalt give the congregation and their beasts drink. And Moses took the rod from before the LORD, as he commanded him. And Moses and Aaron gathered the congregation together before the rock, and he said unto them, Hear now, ye rebels; must we fetch you water out of this rock? And Moses lifted up his hand, and with his rod he smote the rock twice: and the water came out abundantly, and the congregation drank, and their beasts also. **And the LORD spake unto Moses and Aaron, Because ye believed Me not, to sanctify Me in the eyes of the children of Israel, therefore ye shall not bring this congregation into the land which I have given them.**

Consequences Of Doing Evil In God's Sight: David's Son Must Die; Jeroboam's Son Must Die

2-Samuel 12:1-24 And the LORD sent Nathan unto David. And he came unto him, and said unto him, There were two men in one city; the one rich, and the other poor. The rich man had exceeding many flocks and herds: But the poor man had nothing, save one little ewe lamb, which he had bought and nourished up: and it grew up together with him, and with his children; it did eat of his own meat, and drank of his own cup, and lay in his bosom, and was unto him as a daughter. And there came a traveller unto the rich man, and he spared to take of his own flock and of his own herd, to dress for the wayfaring man that was come unto him; but took the poor man's lamb, and dressed it for the man that was come to him. And David's anger was greatly kindled against the man; and he said to Nathan, As the LORD liveth, the man that hath done this thing shall surely die: And he shall restore the lamb fourfold, because he did this thing, and because he had no pity. And Nathan said to David, **Thou art the man.** Thus saith the LORD God of Israel, I anointed thee king over Israel, and I delivered thee out of the hand of Saul; And I gave thee thy master's house, and thy master's wives into thy bosom, and gave thee the house of Israel and of Judah; and if that had been too little, I would moreover have given unto thee such and such things. Wherefore hast thou despised the commandment of the LORD, to do evil in his sight? thou hast killed Uriah the Hittite with the sword, and hast taken his wife to be thy wife, and hast slain him with the sword of the children of Ammon. Now therefore the sword shall never depart from thine house; because thou hast despised me, and hast taken the wife of Uriah the Hittite to be thy wife. Thus saith the LORD, Behold, I will raise up evil against thee out of thine own house, and I will take thy wives before thine eyes, and give them unto thy neighbour, and he shall lie with thy wives in the sight of this sun. For thou didst it secretly: but I will do this thing before all Israel, and before the sun. And David said unto Nathan, I have sinned against the LORD. And Nathan said unto David, The LORD also hath put away thy sin; thou shalt not die. Howbeit, **because by this deed** thou hast given great occasion to the enemies of the LORD to blaspheme, **the child also that is born unto thee shall surely die.** And Nathan departed unto his house. And the LORD struck the child that Uriah's wife bare unto David, and it was very sick. David therefore besought God for the child; and David fasted, and went in, and lay all night upon the earth. And the elders of his house arose, and went to him, to raise him up from the earth: but he would not, neither did he eat bread with them. And it came to pass on the seventh day, that the child died. And the servants of David feared to tell him that the child was dead: for they said, Behold, while the child was yet alive, we spake unto him, and he would not hearken unto our voice: how will he then vex himself, if we tell him that the child is dead? But when David saw that his servants whispered, David perceived that the child was dead: therefore David said unto his servants, Is the child dead? And they said, He is dead. Then David arose from the earth, and washed, and anointed himself, and changed his apparel, and came into the house of the LORD, and worshipped: then he came to his own house; and when he required, they set bread before him, and he did eat. Then said his servants unto him, What thing is this that thou hast done? thou didst fast and weep for the child, while it was alive; but when the child was dead, thou didst rise and eat bread. And he said, **While the child was yet alive, I fasted and wept: for I said, Who can tell whether GOD will be gracious to me, that the child may live? But now he is dead, wherefore should I fast?** can I bring him back again? I shall go to him, but he shall not return to me. And David comforted Bathsheba his wife, and went in unto her, and lay with her: and she bare a son, and he called his name Solomon: and the LORD loved him.

1-Kings 14:1-12, 17-18   At that time Abijah the son of Jeroboam fell sick. And Jeroboam said to his wife, Arise, I pray thee, and disguise thyself, that thou be not known to be the wife of Jeroboam; and get thee to Shiloh: behold, there is Ahijah the prophet, which told me that I should be king over this people. And take with thee ten loaves, and cracknels, and a cruse of honey, and go to him: he shall tell thee what shall become of the child. And Jeroboam's wife did so, and arose, and went to Shiloh, and came to the house of Ahijah. But Ahijah could not see; for his eyes were set by reason of his age. And the LORD said unto Ahijah, Behold, the wife of Jeroboam cometh to ask a thing of thee for her son; for he is sick: thus and thus shalt thou say unto her: for it shall be, when she cometh in, that she shall feign herself to be another woman. And it was so, when Ahijah heard the sound of her feet, as she came in at the door, that he said, Come in, thou wife of Jeroboam; why feignest thou thyself to be another? for I am sent to thee with heavy tidings. Go, tell Jeroboam, Thus saith the LORD God of Israel, **Forasmuch as I exalted thee from among the people, and made thee prince over My people Israel, And rent the kingdom away from the house of David, and gave it thee: and yet thou hast not been as My servant David, who kept My commandments, and who followed Me with all his heart, to do that only which was right in Mine eyes; But hast done evil above all that were before thee: for thou hast gone and made thee other gods, and molten images, to provoke Me to anger, and hast cast Me behind thy back: Therefore, behold, I will bring evil upon the house of Jeroboam,** and will cut off from Jeroboam him that pisseth against the wall, and him that is shut up and left in Israel, and will take away the remnant of the house of Jeroboam, as a man taketh away dung, till it be all gone. Him that dieth of Jeroboam in the city shall the dogs eat; and him that dieth in the field shall the fowls of the air eat: for the LORD hath spoken it. Arise thou therefore, **get thee to thine own house: and when thy feet enter into the city, the child shall die.** And Jeroboam's wife arose, and departed, and came to Tirzah: **and when she came to the threshold of the door, the child died;** And they buried him; and all Israel mourned for him, according to the word of the LORD, which He spake by the hand of His servant Ahijah the prophet.

Proverbs 10:14, 18, 23 Wise men lay up knowledge: but the mouth of the **fool**ish is near destruction. He that hideth hatred with lying lips, and he that uttereth a slander, is a **fool**. It is as sport to a **fool** to do mischief: but a man of understanding hath **wisdom.**

Proverbs 12:15 The way of a **fool** is right in his own eyes: but he that hearkeneth unto counsel is **wise.**

Proverbs 14:1, 7, 16 Every **wise** woman buildeth her house: but the **fool**ish plucketh it down with her hands. Go from the presence of a **fool**ish man, when thou perceivest not in him the lips of **knowledge.** A **wise** man feareth, and departeth from evil: but the **fool** rageth, and is confident.

Proverbs 15:2, 5, 7, 14, 20 The tongue of the **wise** useth knowledge aright: but the mouth of **fool**s poureth out foolishness. A **fool** despiseth his Father's instruction: but he that regardeth reproof is prudent._The lips of the **wise** disperse knowledge: but the heart of the **fool**ish doeth not so. The heart of him that hath understanding seeketh knowledge: but the mouth of **fool**s feedeth on foolishness. A **wise** son maketh a glad Father: but a **fool**ish man despiseth his mother.

Proverbs 17:7, 10, 21, 25, 28 Excellent speech becometh not a **fool**: much less do lying lips a prince. A reproof entereth more into a **wise** man than an hundred stripes into a **fool**. He that begetteth a **fool** doeth it to his sorrow: and the Father of a fool hath no joy. A **fool**ish son is a grief to his Father, and bitterness to her that bare him. Even a **fool**, when he holdeth his peace, is counted **wise.**

Proverbs 18:2, 7 A **fool** hath no delight in understanding, but that his heart may discover itself. A **fool**'s mouth is his destruction, and his lips are the snare of his soul.

Proverbs 19:1, 10, 13 Better is the poor that walketh in his integrity, than he that is perverse in his lips, and is a **fool**. Delight is not seemly for a **fool**; much less for a servant to have rule over princes. A **fool**ish son is the calamity of his Father.

Proverbs 20:3 It is an honour for a man to cease from strife: but every **fool** will be meddling.

Proverbs 23:9 Speak not in the ears of a **fool**: for he will despise the **wisdom** of thy words.

Proverbs 24:7 **Wisdom** is too high for a **fool**.

Proverbs 26:1, 3-5, 9, 11 As snow in summer, and as rain in harvest, so honour is not seemly for a **fool**. A whip for the horse, a bridle for the ass, and a rod for the **fool**'s back. Answer not a **fool** according to his folly, lest thou also be like unto him. Answer a **fool** according to his folly, lest he be **wise** in his own conceit. As a thorn goeth up into the hand of a drunkard, so is a parable in the mouths of **fool**s. As a dog returneth to his vomit, so a **fool** returneth to his folly.

Proverbs 28:26 He that trusteth in his own heart is a **fool**: but whoso walketh **wisely**, he shall be delivered.

Proverbs 29:11 A **fool** uttereth all his mind: but a **wise** man keepeth it in till afterwards.

Psalm 14:1 The **fool** hath said in his heart, There is no God.

2-Timothy 2:23 But **fool**ish and unlearned questions avoid, knowing that they do gender strifes.

Titus 3:9 But avoid **fool**ish questions, and genealogies, and contentions, and strivings about the law; for they are unprofitable and vain.

Revelation 19:20 And the beast was taken, and with him the false prophet that wrought miracles before him, with which he deceived them that had received the mark of the beast, and them that worshipped his image. These both were cast alive into a **Lake of Fire burning with brimstone.**

Revelation 20:10 And the devil that deceived them was cast into the **Lake of Fire and brimstone**, where the beast and the false prophet are, **and shall be tormented day and night for ever and ever.**

Revelation 20:14 And death and hell were cast into the **Lake of Fire**. This is the second death.

Revelation 20:15 And whosoever was not found written in the Book of Life was cast into the **Lake of Fire.**

Revelation 21:8 But the fearful, and unbelieving, and the abominable, and murderers, and whoremongers, and sorcerers, and idolaters, and all liars, shall have their part in the **Lake which burneth with Fire and brimstone**: which is the second death.

"THE MARATHON RACE"

Many songs are written, worldly thoughts in mind,
We wrote this song, our tenth, our tithe.
Many lost persons trying to find the way,
We're here to encourage and show today.

Right words and actions can set you straight.
Life is a marathon, to make it to the gate.
Like any race, you must count up the cost.
Without the right values, you'll surely be lost.

So check out our words, and follow the song,
Make the commitment, you can't go wrong.
The race is not promised to the swift or strong,
But those who endure, and strive for no wrong.
It's a marathon race. It's a marathon race.

Live your life by the golden rule.
Do unto others as you want them to do unto you.
Treat all people with the respect due.
At some time in life, you'll have been there too.

So dedicate some time each day,
To seek him for guidance as you go your own way.
Love thy neighbor as thyself.
The Kingdom can be yours, it gives true wealth.

So promise yourself, to improve yourself,
There'll be no time left, to fault anyone else.
Get the right values, and the race is yours.
Read the Good Book, you'll find the right choice.
It's a marathon race. It's a marathon race.

Marriage will test endurance and plans,
Vows make only a symbol to man.
You've made the real vow, you understand,
To God up above to go the distance if you can.

Find your place in the Master's plan.
Ecclesiastes:12, helps you understand.
Fear God and keep His commandments,
For this is the whole duty of man.

Go the distance with courage and faith.
Run your race, show others the way.
The race is not promised to the swift or strong,
But the person repentant for their wrong.
It's a marathon race. It's a marathon race.

The Father, Holy Ghost, and the Son,
Baptize in their names for the race to be won.
The way to salvation is his only Son.
The race is long, you've just begun.

You must believe in your heart, that He rose the third day.
And confess with your mouth, He has paved the way.
The meek and humble shall inherit the earth.
Pray without ceasing if you want to be first.

Every knee must bow in all humanity,
And confessions made, all is vanity.
Same gift for all who endure the race,
Eternal life and eternal grace.
It's a marathon race.

"IT'S LIKE TRYING TO CATCH THE WIND"

In life, and in death, get right, or get left.

These verses are from the book of Ecclesiastes.
Read it to find your purpose in life in these.
People wonder what life's all about.
Ecclesiastes leaves no doubt, when God is left out.

Written by the wisest man on earth.
Solomon, son of King David, he put God first.
With his great power, he studied knowledge and madness,
He concluded:
The greater your wisdom, the more your sadness.

Without God, things seem to have no rhyme or reason.
With God, everything has its own time and season.
A time to be born, and a time to die.
A time to keep quiet, and a time to cry.

We all face the same destiny when we meet our end.
Life without God, it's like trying to catch the wind.

Remember your Creator when you are young,
Before the days of trouble come.
God will judge everything and everyone.
There is nothing new under the sun.

There will be many dark days over the years,
But live life boldly, and cast aside your fears.
The breath of life enters within a mother's womb.
No one can predict their own death or doom.

A gift from God to serenely accept your situation and fate.
With an attitude of gratitude, praise Him anyway.
God has made the good times as well as the bad.
Only whatever you've done for Christ will last.

We all face the same destiny when we meet our end.
Life without God, it's like trying to catch the wind.

Don't be too wise, and don't be a fool, my brother.
It's good to hold onto one, and not let go of the other.
Do all that you do to His glory with all your might.
Lean not to thine own understanding or sight.

Swift justice is required when people do crimes.
The sea is never full, though rivers flow there all the times.
Righteous people also will die,
While wicked people seem to always get by.

The best thing for people to do under the sun,
Is to eat, drink, and enjoy, everyone.
Our lifelong duty for every woman and man,
Is to try hard as we can,
To fear God and keep His commands.

We all face the same destiny when we meet our end.
Life without God, it's like trying to catch the wind.

Map To The Treasure *(We should apply the following commandments concurrently, consistently, daily.)*

- Never forget the importance of what life is all about: there is joy in the presence of the Angels of God over one sinner that repenteth.
- Acknowledge that there is none other commandment greater than the first two: You must love the Lord thy God with all thy heart, and with all thy soul, and with all thy mind, and with all thy strength; and thou shalt love thy neighbor as thyself. Prioritize Jesus first, neighbors second, and yourself last.
- Judge righteously, remembering that the saints shall judge the world and Angels.
- Ensure that your righteousness exceeds the scribes and Pharisees.
- Seek God's grace and gift of discernment to grant you the serenity to accept the things that you can not change, the courage to change the things that you can, and the wisdom to know the difference.
- Pray without ceasing.
- Pray, Fast, and do charitable deeds in secret to be rewarded openly.
- Remember that Fasting in addition to Praying, yields blessed results.
- Love your enemies, bless those who curse you, do good to those who hate you, and pray for those who spitefully use and persecute you.
- Attend Church Worship; keep your foot when you go to the house of God, and be more ready to hear, than to give the sacrifice of fools.
- Confess the Lord Jesus; believe that God raised Him from the dead.
- Pay Tithes.
- Do not have the *love* of money.
- Be a cheerful giver.
- Keep the commandments; and keep vows and promises.
- Study, meditate and delight in the law of the Lord day and night.

- Praise the Lord; Fear the Lord; Love the Lord; Exalt the Lord; Trust the Lord; Serve the Lord, and Wait on the Lord.
- Preach the word; be instant in season, out of season.
- Remember that His sun will rise on the evil and the good, and His rain will fall on the just and the unjust.
- Redeem your time wisely; seek the Kingdom of God first.
- Be content; glory in our tribulations; avoid coveteousness.
- Remember that eyes have not seen, ears haven't heard, and neither has it entered into the hearts of those, the things which God hath prepared for them who love Him.
- Seek peace, and pursue it; submit to God, and resist the devil.
- Depart from evil, and do good.
- Be meek, poor in spirit, pure in heart, merciful, a peacemaker, plus hunger and thirst after righteousness, in order to be blessed.
- Put on the armour of God; put on the fruit of the Spirit.
- Don't swear or curse.
- Be swift to hear, slow to speak, and slow to anger.
- Be ye angry, and sin not: let not the sun go down upon your wrath; neither give place to the devil.
- If confronting a person who trespassed against you, go and tell them their fault between you and them alone.
- Sing and make melody in your heart to the Lord.
- Honor thy father and mother.
- Seek to establish a good name.
- Avoid foolish questions.
- Set your affection on things above, not on things on the earth.
- Think on these things if there be any virtue or praise: whatsoever things are true, whatsoever things are honest, whatsoever things are just, whatsoever things are pure, whatsoever things are lovely, or whatsoever things are of good report.
- And whatsoever ye do in word or deed, do all in the name of the Lord Jesus, giving thanks to God and the Father by Him; and do it heartily, as to the Lord and not unto men.

- Let your light so shine before men that people will see your good works and glorify your Father in Heaven.
- Treat people right, especially persons poor, homeless, needy, maimed, lame, blind, imprisoned, sick, afflicted, fatherless, widows, or Special Needs.
- Bear ye one another's burdens, and bear the infirmities of the weak.
- Don't mock the poor (or anybody else) and thereby reproach their maker, for we are all the work of His hands.
- Refrain from anything whereby thy brother stumbleth, or is offended, or is made weak.
- Exhort and encourage one another daily.
- Warn persons unruly; comfort the feebleminded; support the weak; be patient toward all men.
- Withhold not good from them to whom it is due, when it is in the power of thine hand to do it.
- Share your possessions like the father of the prodigal son, all is vanity.
- Sacrifice; don't be weary in well-doing.
- Fight the good fight, finish the course, yet nevertheless expect persecution and to be lied against for living your life for Christ.
- Hate the (7) things that God hates: a proud look, a lying tongue, hands that shed innocent blood, an heart that deviseth wicked imaginations, feet that be swift in running to mischief, a false witness that speaketh lies, and he that soweth discord among brethren.
- Develop and practice Faith at all times; Remember Elisha and faith of the Shunammite mother (It is well).
- Develop a strong Faith, remembering that without Faith, it is impossible to please God, for He is a rewarder of them who diligently seek Him.
- Dwell separately, in lieu of divorce.
- Be comforted knowing that the eyes of the Lord are over the righteous, His ears are open unto their prayers: but the face of the Lord is against them that do evil.
- Be persuaded, confident that neither death, nor life, nor angels, nor principalities, nor powers, nor things present, nor things to come, nor height, nor depth, nor any other creature, shall be able to separate us from the love of God, which is in Christ Jesus our Lord.

"THE MAN WHO COULD SEE ANGELS"

**Special bonus book originally written 2008
for spiritual enrichment and encouragement**

**Amazing <u>TRUE</u> Stories
That Will Inspire <u>YOU</u> To Believe
and To See ANGELS Too!!**

Hello Team, welcome to my world, a world where I approach each day expecting to experience miracles, blessings, and ANGELS. ANGELS have always been here, but only recently did I start to notice and acknowledge them. I attribute it to my level of spiritual growth. I don't remember when I first started noticing ANGELS within the last 20 years, but nowadays, I'm sure to quickly acknowledge their presence, and to give God the glory, honor, and praise for having sent them. Acknowledgement of His ANGELS seems to confirm an appreciation to God for His gift, and gives me the reassurance that He will reward me with His divine gift again and again. I started noticing ANGELS more once I opened up my heart to receiving God's will, always mindful of several key scriptures including:

Hebrews 13:2   Be not forgetful to entertain strangers; for thereby some have entertained ANGELS unawares.

Psalm 91:11   For he shall give his ANGELS charge over thee, to keep thee in all thy ways.

Most people have a perception and visualize that ANGELS are winged persons dressed in white clothing with an ever-present glowing halo suspended beautifully over their head. Perhaps the ones from Heaven are like that, but let me give you my definition regarding the ANGELS that I see all the time, because I've come to the conclusion that: **An ANGEL is an ordinary person that God uses in an extra-ordinary way, time, or place, to have a significant positive impact on someone's life, to do His will.**

Perhaps after you read the true stories in this book, you will start to remember the times that you have also experienced ANGELS in your life. Think about the times that someone may have helped you through a difficult situation, or made a significant difference to overcome an extremely tough adversity or adversary, and then you will realize that you may have seen ANGELS too! We all know that God works in mysterious ways, but have you ever thought about the idea that "YOU" are His mysterious ways? I've noticed that God uses "ordinary" people in His own "extra-ordinary" way, time or place to do His will and serve His purposes. Each situation allows God's love and presence to be made manifest in everyday people, who usually unknowingly serve as His ANGELS. So as you can imagine, I am not the only Man Who Could See ANGELS; YOU DO TOO!! ANGELS come in all sizes; short or tall, young or old, slender or full-figured, Black or White, rich or poor, sinner or saint. But one thing that I've noticed is that they always seem to have a cheerful countenance and a smile on their face.

By the way, on another subject, have you ever noticed the phenomenon that whenever one person yawns, that it seems contagious, and another person will also yawn? I've got my own theory about the cause, and I'm going to hold fast to my presumption until proven otherwise: I think that a heavenly ANGEL passed in the midst and touched both lives. If you have a more plausible reason, then please let me know.

167

When You Are The Angel

The realization that you might be handling something in the capacity of an ANGEL, that you may therefore be representing God, should make a person hold themselves to a higher standard. Even greater emphasis should be placed on ensuring that Christian values are espoused at all times. Whenever you may perform a good deed, you should strive to not accept any reciprocal gift, reward, or gratuities. But instead, you should mention that all of the glory, honor, and praise should go to Him who you serve as His humble servant.

For example, if you help someone with something, and they offer to give you an earthly $10, you should not accept it because the heavenly treasure that you will build up instead and the heavenly blessings that you may receive instead, would probably be ten-fold greater than whatever a mortal person could offer. Also, the heavenly treasure that you would build up would extend to your children and your children's children, even to the 3rd and 4th generation.

Sometimes, it may be unavoidable to receive credit for your good deeds, but whenever you're tempted to **intentionally** receive personal glory, honor, praise, or compensation for good/righteous deeds performed as God's humble servant, just always remember Moses' fate. If I am permitted to embellish, Moses was God's "main man", because he is the only man who ever walked and talked with God. Moses did all the signs and wonders which the Lord sent him to do to the Pharaoh of Egypt, brought forth the ten plagues, parted the Red Sea, and led the children of Israel for more than 40 years, serving God faithfully. When God's people asked for water in the desert, God made it possible by telling Moses to speak to/strike the rock with the rod to cause water to flow. However, Moses gave the people the impression that he was the hero for getting water for them, thereby receiving the glory and praise that was rightfully due to the almighty God. God therefore banned Moses from going into the Promised Land. He allowed Moses to see it from afar, but did not let him set foot in the land. The moral of the story is that if God "zapped" His "main man" who had

168

faithfully served Him for more than 40 years, due to Moses' transgression or temporary insubordination, then you can imagine what He may do to you or me, if we were to seek the glory that is rightfully due to Him. God is not a respecter of persons.

Let's Set The Stage

Let me set the stage for the collection of true stories that I am about to share with you. These experiences are from my (66) years of life; from being the 9th out of (13) children; from (48) years of marriage to my bride Juanita; from my epic (40) years GM employment (now retired); from having raised (4) children (David Jr. – 46, Steven – 45, Davena – 38, and Andrew – 34); from being the Manager of QTMC hip-hop/rap music group for (30) years; from being the Manager of CENTERSTAGE Banquet Rental Hall (homeless shelter) for (19) years; and from my vehicles (1995 Chevrolet Suburban and 2005 Pontiac Montana) breaking down on the expressway several times during the grueling 12-hour journey frequently driven back and forth to our hometown of Winston-Salem, North Carolina. My activities and travels have taken me all over the USA and Canada. Along the way, I've met many ANGELS, and I would like to share some of those experiences with you. I have intentionally omitted any references which may have included family members (except for my Mom), for fear of alienating those that I may not have mentioned. And of course, I have not shown any specific company names, or individuals' last names, to ensure their privacy. The situations written about in this book are recollections of where someone may have rescued me from a difficult situation.

My First Best Work Friend (9-8-1969)

The beginning of my General Motors tenure is where I would like to start my story. Although I didn't know it initially, it was the beginning of a new mandate at that time, and I was about to be the beneficiary of what I didn't learn until later was called Affirmative Action. In 1968 in the USA, upon high school graduation, most young 18-year-olds were being "drafted" to go to the Vietnam War. So since it seemed inevitable, I decided to prepare myself by becoming skilled to work on our Army tank engines instead of having to be on the front lines. I enrolled in a Diesel Maintenance course at Forsyth Technical Institute in Winston-Salem, NC. One day, a man came to our class and then discussed something out in the hall with the class Instructor. The Instructor came back into the class and summoned me out into the hall so we could have a short 3-person conference. The man told me that if I should finish that course, then I could get a job with General Motors. Being color-blind regarding Race, I didn't realize the significance at that time, that he had chosen me because I was the only Minority in the class of (50) guys. So I finished the 2nd, 3rd, and 4th quarters of school, and the next month after receiving my diploma in Diesel Maintenance, I went to work for General Motors at the Winston-Salem GMC Truck Center factory store. Still pioneering the way, I was the first Minority mechanic that they had ever hired. I remember always trying to change our shop radio to my favorite station, but I was outnumbered about 40 to 1, so I acquiesced and fell in love with Country Music as you can imagine. For the eight years that I progressed in experience from Helper- to Utility- to Journeyman-Mechanic, some of the fellows were staunchly determined to never accept me, the new kid on the block. However, there was a young mechanic named Doug who befriended me and I became his protégé. He taught me everything about being a mechanic, unselfishly not holding back on anything. He even taught me how to take the engine out of my Chevrolet Corvair and rebuild it on the kitchen table in my apartment. Doug was even persecuted and ostracized by several of the other mechanics for mentoring me, the new young inept rookie. But under his tutorage, I became a progressively better

171

mechanic, a better man, and a better person in life from the many values instilled in me from being a mechanic. Besides learning how to be a good mechanic, I also learned such characteristics as patience, motivation, stick-to-it-iveness, determination, confidence, competence, friendliness, and integrity. After being a mechanic for (8) years, I was a Retail Truck Salesman for (2) years before I spent the last (30) years of my GM career in Zone Office & Home Office Fleet Departments. If Doug had not taken me under his wings to set me on the right path (40) years ago, then I seriously doubt if I could have written this book. Doug is an ANGEL.

My Mentor Adopted My Family   (1-1-1978)

When I transferred to the Charlotte Zone office, I was a novice, eager to learn all about Zone and Home Office policies and procedures. Some people in life will help you just so you will go away, and some people will help you because they are genuinely concerned. A man named Gordon befriended me and would go the extra mile to ensure that I was handling matters in a quality way. He knew that if I was going to make it in this white-collar world, then there would be several things that I needed to always strive to get right. Since taking me under his wings about (31) years ago, I have far exceeded most of my lifetime expectations, largely due to the apprenticeship and tutoring that I got from Gordon. And then I met his wife Marion, and was pleasantly surprised to find out that she was just as nice as Gordon! Over the years, they have not only seemingly adopted me and my family, but they act like the surrogate parents to many of their friend's/family's children. They have been closer than a brother. My wife and I will forever cherish their friendship. I can not think of enough superlatives to describe our admiration and gratefulness for the kindness and love that they have showered upon me and our family. Every Labor Day for the last (27) years, many of Gordon and Marion's friends and family have joined them at their Romp-N-Stomp family recreational weekend at their retreat in the Virginia mountains. Some people camp out in the big field, and then we engage in activities such as volley ball, skeet shooting (couldn't believe that my wife and I have actually shot real shotguns), target practice with bows and arrows, riding motorcross motorcycles, digging for potatoes, and playing in the creek. We stuff ourselves on an abundance of food, and overall we always experience a simply fantastic time. "To the world, you might be one person, but to one person you might be the whole world". Gordon and Marion are my heroes, and for sure they are ANGELS.

Our First Home   **(12-1-1984)**

General Motors had transferred my employment from Charlotte, North Carolina to Pontiac, Michigan, so I was about to start driving northbound that morning. My previous Zone Office partner Kurt kindly asked me to stop by his home for breakfast as I drove through his hometown of Mt. Airy on the way to Michigan. After a fantastic breakfast, Kurt's wife Ramona told me to visit a certain realtor whenever I reached town, and I thought that was an insignificant suggestion at that time. Upon arrival in Pontiac, Michigan, I sought that realtor, and they ultimately sold us our first home. In my previous four job transfers with General Motors, we had always remained flexible to move by renting apartments or townhouses. But finally, we had put down some roots and purchased our first home, which likely would not have happened if I had not happened to stop for breakfast. Kurt and Ramona were ANGELS.

Sometimes, if an employee wants to do the best that they can on their job, they will read and often refer to their job function's instruction manual. Likewise, to do the best that we can in our job of life itself, many of us read our manual as often as we can for guidance. My King James has a fitting acronym, "Basic Instructions Before Leaving Earth", of course, the BIBLE. The BIBLE is the foundation upon which my faith and integrity is built and grows.

We had congregated for our weekly lunch hour at-work Bible Study. A fellow worker named Joyce was sent into my life to emphasize the passages which are essential for a person to know in order to feel reassured of their salvation while diligently seeking spiritual direction:

1. **Romans 10:9** That if thou shalt confess with thy mouth the Lord Jesus, and shalt believe in thine heart that God hath raised him from the dead, thou shalt be saved.

2. **Ephesians 4:30** And grieve not the Holy Spirit of God, whereby we are sealed unto the day of redemption.

With that reassurance, that was the day that I accepted Jesus Christ as my spiritual savior. That was a special day, a momentous day that put me on a never-ending journey to seek His face. It awakened and heightened a keen awareness in me, that ultimately, life is all about preparation for death and where your soul will spend eternity.

Our First Corporate Sponsor   (12-15-1988)

My son Steve and his friend Milton wrote a song called My Buddie, and began to rap it in several talent shows around town, and always received rave reviews. With the skills that had been awakened by that song, Steve then began to rap other positive motivational raps over the school's loudspeaker each day. They called themselves "QTMC", and I was designated the Manager, and we were invited to perform at City Hall in Pontiac for the Red Ribbon Campaign. That was the momentous day that our lives became enriched when we caught the eye of a lady named Jackie, who was the Public Relations Manager for a major corporation. She offered to sponsor us to go to selected schools and stores to perform concerts for her. With our first major corporate sponsor, we eventually performed at about (300) high schools, corporate stores, and at a Census 1980 Convention in California for our sponsor. That launched our music career and gave us the motivation and confidence to know that we could eventually reach our potential. The experience gained from working with Jackie taught us how to become free lance artists. As a result, we have performed about (1,200) motivational youth concerts career-to-date. Jackie was an ANGEL.

Teachers Deserve A Standing Ovation   (12-15-1988)

When QTMC was performing at the Red Ribbon Campaign event at Pontiac's City Hall, I also met a nice young lady named Pam who used to be a teacher, but has since taken on the greater responsibility of collaborating with (900) Jr./Sr. High Schools in Michigan, and little did I know that she would also change our lives forever. Over the years, we have since developed a close working relationship as she has been directly influential in QTMC performing about (500) concerts. Through her association with the (900) Michigan Middle Schools and High Schools, she has endorsed and promoted QTMC because we have always strived to do a quality job for her and made each motivational youth concert a successful event. She has demonstrated exemplary leadership in her dedication to encourage young people to make the right decisions in their lives by adopting a drug free life style. She has worked closely with the largest student-led youth group in schools for about 25 years. She is a fantastic role model and brings joy, confidence, and reassurance to everyone around her. She is a very special person, and has demonstrated kindness in many ways over the years: such as when she downsized and relocated her office and therefore blessed our fledgling charity with various desks, tables, and chairs. Also, when her father's family business was relocated, she also donated various building furniture. Pam has always been very supportive of our Charity, and we are very grateful. She has enabled our QTMC Music Group many opportunities to grow by featuring us to her Michigan-state-wide 900-school student body. Also, as a fellow small business owner, I've learned much from her. We have the utmost respect for Pam, and value her friendship greatly. She is one of my heroes, and I've told her that "no matter how high I get, I'll still be looking up to you." She has always been the ultimate teacher. Pam is an ANGEL.

Navy Furlough In Mississippi   (10-31-1989)

When my son David Jr. was in the Navy, he was trying to go home on military leave to his wife in Mississippi. He asked me for assistance, but being financially challenged as I often was, I called a dealership in New Orleans and spoke with a man named Santo to seek his advice on a loaner vehicle. He said that he could not loan me a vehicle, but he could sell me a good used vehicle, that I could elect to return in one week if I changed my mind. We therefore coordinated all of the arrangements and he picked up my son at the airport, and David Jr. signed the contract for me to purchase a like-new 1985 light blue Chevrolet Impala that he drove during his Navy leave. A week later, Santo obligingly rescinded the contract, accepted the car back and drove David Jr. back to the airport. He was very kind and understanding, and he never charged me a penny. Without him, David Jr. may not have been able to come home from Desert Storm at that time. Through our telephone communications and his kind assistance, I could tell that Santo was an ANGEL.

Just Sign Here

In 1997, it seemed like everything was going wrong in my life: We were having marriage problems; we were having financial problems; and plus we had just been robbed at home. Thieves had kicked our doors in and robbed our home of many valuables, particularly our QTMC music equipment, which had exacerbated my financial woes. Meanwhile, my son Steve was persistently badgering me to try to lease this vacated hall in town so we could convert it into a teen dance center. I'll bet that I told him "No" more than (20) times, but he still persisted. In order to get him off my case, I finally relented and said "Okay, we'll have a meeting with the Investment Company, but don't expect anything to come of it because they're probably going to say that we're too broke". Steve set up the meeting, and we met with the Investment Company owners Jim and his son/partner Greg. You can imagine my surprise when they essentially said "Just Sign Here", and that we would negotiate the financing. Wow! When we left that meeting, we jumped for joy! Since then, our business relationship has strengthened and grown to where we're now partners in another business venture. If they had not taken a chance on us, and given us the opportunity to prove ourselves by operating our small business CENTERSTAGE Rental Hall, Recording Studio, and Homeless Shelter, our lives would be on entirely different paths. Their faith in us has directly positively influenced hundreds of lives and souls with the church that we rent to for worship services, and the hundreds of homeless persons that we have provided refuge and meals for the last twelve years. Jim and Greg are ANGELS.

Out Of Gas In West Virginia Mountains   (4-5-1999)

When I purchased my 1995 Suburban from one of my previous truck dealers in North Carolina and started driving back home to Michigan, I was steady enjoying my new toy and didn't bother to notice the fuel gauge since I knew that I had a 40-gallon tank. So after about six hours of driving, I was cruising my usual (75) mph down the mountains of West Virginia, when all of a sudden my engine wouldn't accelerate. Being a mechanic, I didn't panic, but shifted my transmission to neutral, put on my 4-way flasher, then moved to the right lane, and afterwards to the shoulder of the highway, but never touched the brakes until I could coast as far as I could in order to walk to the closest gas station. By the time I finally came to a stop, there was a blue light behind me. Oh no, I hope that I won't get a ticket! The officer said that this was his territory, so he knew that the next gas station was too far ahead to walk. Imagine my relief when he said that he would take me to get some gas! So I got into the trooper's car and we drove across the median and back southbound to a little hardware store in the rural mountains. They handed me a gas can, so I filled it up, and went back and sat down in the passenger seat of the squad car. I remember the trooper's chuckle as he glanced his eyes over at me and said "Are you going to pay for that, or are you going to steal it?" I was so happy that he had gotten me out of the crisis that I had forgotten to pay for the can or the gas! Of course, I ran back inside the store and paid for it, and the trooper drove me back to my Suburban. He saved me from having to potentially walk many miles in those dangerous West Virginia mountains. That State Trooper was an ANGEL.

Alternator Failure In Ohio   (7-17-1999)

There was another time that my son David Jr. and I were driving from North Carolina back to Michigan, and we were going through New Philadelphia, Ohio on the expressway when the engine quit and a quick glimpse at the voltmeter gage indicated that I probably had an alternator problem. Since David Jr. was driving at that moment, I was barking out some fast instructions as we exited and coasted through several stop signs as we headed towards a shopping center. When we finally came to a stop, unbelievably we were right in front of a parts store. Expecting a miracle, sure enough they had another alternator and fan belt in stock. The final hurdle was that I did not have my tool kit with me at that time, so I asked the Parts Store man to loan me the necessary tools. I put the new alternator on my Suburban in about twenty minutes, and returned the borrowed tools. A challenging situation was made easier because of him. That Parts Store man was an ANGEL.

Dallas, Texas Clothes For Church   (9-19-1999)

My experience in Texas profoundly changed my life. Being an avid Dallas Cowboys fanatic, my son Andrew, his friend Deonate, and I planned our vacation around attending a "live" NFL football game.

My 16-year old son Andrew, his best friend Deonate, and I had saved our money to fly from Detroit down to Dallas, Texas to see "America's Team", my Dallas Cowboys (Andrew has since become a die-hard Colts fan). That was the best 4-day vacation of my life!! We strategically got our motel across the expressway from Texas stadium in Irving, Texas. We arrived on Friday, and we planned to just "wing it" and have fun until we would attend the game which would be televised on Monday Night Football.

Being a GM man, the Dallas Zone Office had provided me with a luxurious brand new Cadillac to drive and evaluate. So we visited the Cowboys Training Camp, Main Offices, and Texas Stadium (where we got a memento banner that reads "GM Official Sponsor – Dallas Cowboys Vehicles". We also shopped the malls; we bought official Cowboys Jerseys and souvenirs; we went bowling; we went to the movies; we went swimming; we shot pool (I won); we watched TV; we stuffed ourselves eating to our stomach's desire; and we got very little sleep.

And then came Sunday morning, and it was time to go to church. I'm a self-starter like the Energizer Bunny; I keep going, and going, and going. So I had gotten dressed first in my suit and necktie, before I then woke up Andrew and Deonate to tell them to get ready also. Of course, they said that they had not packed any Sunday clothes, trying to get out of going to church. But being an "old school" person, I had come prepared like a Boy Scout with extra shirts. I told the fellows to put on my two blue oxford-style shirts along with their blue jeans. I told them that they would probably look out of place, but reminded them that we had been blessed with a safe airplane journey and experienced a wonderful vacation, so "fellows, I don't know where we're going, but we're on our way, because we're going to church".

We left our motel in Irving and started driving eastbound on the expressway towards Dallas. When we saw an upcoming exit called Martin L. King Blvd., I said "looks like we're in the neighborhood now." So we drove down that avenue until I saw a street called Malcolm-X Blvd. I said, "We're definitely in the 'hood now". Still searching aimlessly for a potential church to attend worship at, I noticed a church which included the familiar "Missionary Baptist Church", so I told the fellows that we had reached our destination.

So, we went into the church expecting to feel out of place with Andrew and Deonate in blue jeans and oxford shirts. Guess what? It was that church's 60th anniversary, and almost **everyone** was wearing blue jeans and oxford shirts!! I felt like I was walking in lockstep with God!! Out of all the churches on this planet, God had ordered our steps to a place where we were right in sync with his plans for us. Of course after the sermon, we were able to fellowship with them for the rest of that day, on a fantastic feast and great chicken. That day, my three daily expectations were met: miracles, blessings, and ANGELS.

Tire Store On Stephenson Highway   (2-24-2001)

One cold, winter day, it was snowing like crazy and I was running late and frantically loading up our music equipment for QTMC to perform a concert at a school in Detroit. After I got all of the equipment loaded, finally I headed southbound on I-75, and had just passed the Big Beaver Road exit when I heard a rear tire explode on the Suburban! I was really getting stressed out then because we were already running late for the concert, and the entire program depended on my music equipment and microphones. So I immediately took the next exit Stephenson Highway, looking for any type of shop to fix my tire in the foot-deep snow with the blizzard still pelting us. I coasted into a franchised tire company store, and convinced the shop foreman of my urgent dilemma. He was very kind and understanding, so he gave my truck top priority, fixed my truck and had me back on the road in about twenty minutes. Due to his prompt assistance, we were able to get to the school and set up our music equipment and microphones for the event right on time. We could not have done it without him. That Shop Foreman was an ANGEL.

Shanty Creek Wrong Weekend   (11-2-2002)

There is a high school student leadership group which usually hosts its annual statewide conference each year at the Shanty Creek Resort in upper Michigan a couple hundred miles from our hometown of Pontiac, and my QTMC Music Group usually performs a motivational youth concert for the hundreds of youth attendees. Earlier in that year, organizers had asked me to "save the date", which I did. But unknown to us, while planning the event, the date had been changed by them to the subsequent weekend. Unfortunately, we were never notified of that change and we therefore loaded up three carloads of QTMC members and music equipment and drove the 4-hour epic journey only to realize that it was the wrong weekend! What a bummer!! Acting on faith, I sought the organizers of the financial group who was having their banquet there at that time, and the two brothers' names were Wayne and Les. I asked them if could we perform for them, and emphasized that we would be grateful to accept whatever compensation that they deemed worthy. So not only did they grant us permission to perform a music concert for them on such short notice, but they also compensated us enough to make the trip worthwhile. I was glad that our motivational youth concert format has great crossover appeal even for adults. They saved me from a huge embarrassment, and we were very grateful for them. Wayne and Les were ANGELS.

Flat Tire At Ohio Turnpike Tollbooth   (11-29-2002)

During a trip to North Carolina, instead of making the journey in the Suburban, we were driving in my wife's Montana Van. On the Ohio Turnpike that night, all of a sudden we heard a big KABOOM!   Oh oh, flat tire! We pulled over at the toll booth where there was some light in order to see how to change it. That's when I discovered my real dilemma since we had never changed the tire before on this newly-acquired van. What a time to find out that the lug nut wrench that we had received with the vehicle didn't even fit the van's wheels! So there we were at this seemingly deserted outpost of a toll booth exit from the Ohio Turnpike, one lady attendant, dark at night, cold weather, and **no** lug wrench. So I asked the lady if was there any chance that she had a lug wrench, and surprisingly she said "maybe". She was the driver of a Montana Van just like mine, so we looked to see if she had a lug wrench. Voila!!   She had the factory lug wrench and it worked perfectly to repair my Montana Van, and then we continued on our journey. That lady saved us the time and expense of calling for a wrecker. That toll booth lady was an ANGEL.

Best Insurance Agent In The World   (12-1-2002)

As you can imagine, sometimes the requirements to maintain insurance on a fleet of family vehicles can become overwhelming, and that's what happened to me as I was determining how to prevent a lapse in auto insurance coverage due to my limited finances. I was filled with despair until I got on the phone with a lady named Mary, and she graciously took the time to explain the choices facing me in order to advise the most beneficial avenue to proceed. She handled my situation with the utmost professionalism, dedication, spirit of teamwork, caring, and experience. She was exemplary in her efforts to show compassion and understanding, and I was treated like a friend, rather than just simply as another customer. She not only saved my auto insurance from being cancelled, but also set up my homeowner insurance also. Mary was an ANGEL.

Animal Lover (4-5-2003)

My friend Pam is recognized city-wide for the significant impact that she has on the lives of animals in our area. Pam lives a lifestyle of exemplary dedication and sacrifice and she "sets the standard" for proper animal care. She is to be commended for her tireless efforts to improve the environment for the dogs and cats of our county, and she has cheerfully sacrificed to volunteer her time and service to others. For the last 16 years, Pam has conducted about 51,000 visits to homes in Pontiac to ensure that animals are not being abused, neglected or forced to be fighters, and to educate families, and distribute food, water, doghouses, straw, and other supplies. She has rescued about 9,500 animals, sterilized about 3,200 animals, and vaccinated about 13,000 animals for low/no cost. She has hosted her cats and dogs Vaccination Clinics each April and October at our CENTERSTAGE building and parking lot, and each clinic has been a phenomenal success resulting in hundreds of vaccinations and dog licenses being issued each time. One time she coordinated for the entire medical class from a Michigan university to live with us for three whole days. They set up an actual "M.A.S.H." unit hospital and operated on dozens of animals, and we collaborated with another local hall to provide housing accommodations. That experience really, really, was amazing. Since I met Pam, she has also coordinated her animal-lover friends to donate some of their time and resources to assist us with feeding the homeless/needy all winter. She is the best friend of animals that I have ever met. Pam is an ANGEL.

Broken Fan Belt On I-75 Expressway   (12-1-2004)

I received my diploma in Diesel Maintenance from Forsyth Technical Institute in Winston-Salem, North Carolina in August of 1969, and the next month started as a mechanic in my career at General Motors. I was a salaried worker for the last (30) years, but with the mechanical knowledge that I developed in the first (10) years of my career, I have rescued scores of people in distressed/broken down vehicles dozens of times over the last (40) years. I'm sure that most of them would attest to the fact that I was God's ANGEL at that time. It has been a way of life for me to help get any broken down vehicle off the road, particularly if the vehicle is in likely danger of being hit by another motorist. I recall the time that I was going to work at the GM Global Headquarters in Detroit driving I-75 Expressway southbound, and as I zoomed up the 4-lane McNichols hill at my usual (75) miles per hour, I was shocked to jet past a vehicle stalled in the fast lane and the man was standing in front of the vehicle on the highway! So I took the very next exit, drove Woodward Avenue back northbound, and got back on the expressway to come up behind the broken down vehicle and park with my emergency hazard lights on for protection. The man said that he was scared and had been in this crisis for about (20) minutes, but nobody had stopped to help him. So I took my flashlight from my Suburban, waved it to stop the (2) lanes of I-75 traffic beside his broken down truck, and we pushed his truck to the somewhat-safety of the cement median, and then I took the broken fan belt off. That was his first week as a new teacher in Detroit, so I let him use my cell phone to call in late for work. Because it was about 7:00am, and the Parts Stores were not open yet, I treated him to McDonald's breakfast to help time go by faster. Then, we went to the Parts Store when it finally opened, and fortunately they had the fan belt in stock, so I purchased the fan belt and we headed back to the expressway. With my ever-handy tools combined with my mechanical abilities, while hundreds of vehicles were whizzing by us dangerously on the side of the expressway, I put the new fan belt on the truck. Since he said that he was commuting from Flint to Detroit, and he had not gotten a paycheck yet, my final deed was to donate a few dollars to him for gas. Throughout that entire morning, the man expressed sincere gratitude, as I reminded him that I was merely God's agent sent to him at that time. Without my sacrifice to be late for work myself that morning, he may have been killed on that dangerous expressway. Now that I reflect back, I was the Good Samaritan ANGEL that day.

Our Acapulco Latino Friends   (12-24-2004)

Since we opened our rental hall back in 1997, we mostly operated our business predominantly as a teen center. We've tried all types of media to advertise and promote, but still, business was slow. Then this lady named Maria rented from me, and business started booming. She was sending us so much business that I later learned that everyone referred to our hall as "Maria's Hall". I was flattered that everyone loved our hall, and the rentals were keeping us busy. And for many of those rentals, the decorator for those traditional events such as Baptisms, Wedding Showers, Baby Showers, Mis Quince Anos, Mother's Day, and Ladies Only Nights Out, was usually a nice young man named Alfredo. Maria and Alfredo both became my Latino translators, and have been directly instrumental in us renting about (50) times to the Latino population in our area. Without their endorsement, we would have to return to teen dances as a means to generate revenue. That would be more lucrative, but far more dangerous, because teenagers don't come to see a good dance; they come to see a good fight. Teenagers considered it a badge of honor to have their fight at the hall, so we had to discontinue teen dances. Maria and Alfredo are loyal friends, and have really helped our rental business to flourish despite teen dances. Maria and Alfredo have been ANGELS.

Alternator Failure On NY/NJ Turnpike   (1-3-2005)

My son Steve and I were transporting some tires in my Suburban to our friend Jerome in New York. For the first (10) hours, everything was okay until we stopped to pay the toll on the New York / New Jersey Turnpike. My engine shut down, and smoke began billowing from under the hood. I knew we were in trouble because it was dark at night, snowing, and my alternator had apparently failed. We pushed my truck over to the side of the road while I considered my options. Fortunately for us, there was another car on the side of the road, waiting for her carpool rider. She peeped out the barely open windows of her locked car doors to tell us strangers that there was a gas station at the next exit. I pondered my strategy knowing that I only had enough battery power left to hobble straight to that gas station. So we cranked up, and with no headlights due to lack of battery power, I hurriedly made it to the gas station and parked where lights could shine under my hood while I determined the severity of the repair. As people drove up for gas, I boldly asked about (10) different men for assistance until one man named John finally said yes. Since it was about 7:00pm, he got on his cell phone to call around for me to see what parts store might still be open. Steve stayed with the Suburban while John drove me over to the next town about (10) miles away, where we arrived just before 8:00pm closing time. He waited while I purchased the new alternator and fan belt, and then he drove me back to the Suburban. I had my tools with me, so I installed the new alternator in about (20) minutes, and we continued on our journey. The next day, we went to the New York Knicks game at Madison Square Garden, and Jerome also had two more tickets for John and his daughter. Without John to the rescue, we likely would have had wrecker and hotel expenses compounded with the problem of delay to repair it that next day. John was an ANGEL.

Transmission Failure In WV Mountains   (3-17-2005)

About Memorial Day of 2005, my sisters called me and said that Mom (87 years old), was deathly ill in the hospital, and the doctors said that death was imminent, so I should hurry home to North Carolina. So, my wife Diane, my son David Jr., and I set out on the journey in my Suburban. When we were traveling through the West Virginia mountains, Diane had given me a break by driving for a few hours. Suddenly I heard her say that she was mashing the gas hard as she could, but the truck was not accelerating at all. I immediately told her to not hit the brakes so that we could coast as far as we could. We got happy when we noticed an exit coming up. So with my coaching, and Diane barely touching the brakes, we navigated into a little dirt parking lot on Medina Road. After we stopped, I got under the helm of the steering wheel to diagnose the problem, and sure enough, the transmission was full of fluid but still inoperable. Right then I told Diane and David Jr., "We need an ANGEL". David Jr. and I had both been trying to call a wrecker for about (5) minutes on both of our cell phones when, right on queue, (2) men drove up because that happened to be the local Park-N-Ride lot. I explained our dilemma to the Park-N-Ride rider and surprisingly, his cell phone worked, so he called us a wrecker. That Park-N-Ride rider was our first ANGEL that evening. The wrecker driver arrived and wanted to take us to the closest gas station, but I had him to take us back northbound to the closest GM dealer about (20) miles away. It was a Saturday evening, and I didn't have a plan; all I had was faith, and the constant daily expectation of miracles, blessings, and ANGELS. I had resolved to the fact that we probably were going to spend that night in a motel, and that my other (12) sisters and brothers may be by my mothers side if she were to go on to Glory, and everyone would be wondering why I was absent. When we got to the dealership to park my Suburban in the shop's parking lot, I noticed the janitor working late. I asked him if there was a remote chance that he might have the dealership owner's home phone number. He did!! Wow!! He said that he usually never worked that late on Saturday, but extra details had kept him there. He didn't know it, but he was my second ANGEL for that day.

Armed with the dealer's phone number, I called him and left a phone message. My hopes dimmed as I began wondering if he would promptly call back right then, or when business hours would come again two days later on Monday morning. But then he called before the wrecker had finished parking my Suburban by his shop door! The dealer remembered me from when I used to work in the Winston-Salem GMC Truck Center and the Charlotte Zone Office, so he said that he was coming right over to his dealership. When he arrived and became aware of our dilemma, we went out to his Used Truck Lot and picked out a white Suburban that had been on Daily Rental, so it was like brand new. All of this drama happened over about an hour and one/half, and then we were back on the road as if we had not skipped a beat. Without the dealer loaning me that Suburban, and also allowing flexible payments on that $1400 transmission repair bill, I would not have been able to visit Mom when she was very ill. The doctors were wrong anyway; Mom's health improved and she remained feisty as ever in her old folk's home for almost four more years. That dealer was my third ANGEL that Saturday night.

Chairs For Rental Hall (4-15-2005)

For each banquet hall rental as our business began to boom, it was a challenge to have enough tables and chairs for our ever-increasing customer population. One Saturday, I was especially getting stressed out because I had run out of chairs, and couldn't find anyplace to borrow or rent chairs. I got into my Suburban, and got ready to drive off my parking lot in search of chairs, when I noticed Shirley, the lady that we had just DJ'd for the previous week, sitting at the stoplight in her truck. I drove up beside her and quickly mentioned my predicament, and was pleasantly surprised to hear her say that she might have the solution to my problem! Shirley helped me to contact the same hall where we had just DJ'd the prior week, and they donated about (100) chairs to us because they had just bought new chairs! Because of her involvement, I've never had a shortage of chairs since that time. Shirley was an ANGEL.

Jonathan Needs An Angel   (5-15-2005)

One day I was helping my friend Jonathan to move some furniture into his home. It was tricky trying to get the big items and appliances into the basement without damaging the walls. Sure enough, we hit an impasse where we couldn't go any further because the desk was too heavy and cumbersome. So, I told Jonathan right then "We need an ANGEL, so I'm going to go and get us an ANGEL". I went outside to the 2-lane service drive next to the home, and browsed oncoming cars in order to flag down some help. Within about 5 minutes, a car stopped to see what the problem was. I told him of our situation trying to move some heavy furniture, and how we were stuck and needed his help. He said that he would be glad to oblige. That guy was a weight lifter, so he was glad to flex his muscles. He lifted the desk and made it look so easy. A lot of people could have stopped to help, but take notice that God knew that not only did I need an ANGEL, but we needed a **strong** ANGEL, so He sent us exactly who we needed. That situation also reaffirmed my faith in knowing that God actually hears and answers the prayers of those striving to be His humble servants. That strong young man was an ANGEL.

Flat Tire On I-696 Expressway   (12-1-2005)

One cold winter morning, I was driving I-75 Expressway to work in Detroit, and the detour forced motorists from I-75 to I-696 Expressway. So, as I zipped around that exit ramp, I couldn't believe it as traffic was just barely missing this man trying to change his flat tire. So I took the next exit and navigated the streets up Woodward until I could drive up again behind the stranded motorist. It was below freezing cold, and he had stripped out the lug nuts trying to get the flat tire off. So we got back in my Suburban and went to the Auto Parts store on Woodward. I over-bought $150 worth of sockets, wrenches, lubricants, gloves, and everything that we might possibly need in order to get that tire fixed the first-time around, because it was too cold and too dangerous for wasting any time on that expressway. So using all of the ingenuity and experience that I could muster, I finally got enough grip on the stripped lug nuts in order to break them loose. Finally, despite the dangerous location, below-freezing temperature, and stripped lug nuts, we got the tire changed and that man said that he was very grateful as he went on his way. I had deliberately not given him my name or number while we worked on this project for more than an hour, instead trying to emphasize that God deserved the praise for sending me his way. But finally I gave him my name. About a year later, someone called me to ask for a hall rental like usual, but although I insisted that they could get the hall's address when he would arrive to rent from me in person, he was persistent until I gave him the address over the phone. A few days later, I received a check for $40 as a token of appreciation. I called the person who sent the check to ask who he was, and he refreshed my memory about that cold morning on the expressway. To him, I was the Good Samaritan ANGEL that day.

Computer Failure

Let me tell you about the frustrating experience with my computer. One evening I was working on an important document when a thunderstorm caused a community-wide electrical blackout. When the power was restored, my computer failed to boot up. In the next several days, as I tried to get it repaired, I received the same answer from three different computer stores: that they could replace my hard drive for about $1,000, but it would cause me to lose all my important data. That answer was unacceptable of course so I continued to search for a 4th opinion. I decided to try a Computer store over in Keego Harbor. The technician named David was a very kind young man, and he filled me with hope that my data was salvageable. With the possible imminent loss of my computer data, and expecting some ridiculous proposed price for service charges looming for the entire ordeal, I was extremely surprised when David called me early the next morning and said that he had repaired the computer with no loss of data, and my bill was only $49! I have never had anymore problems from my computer since then. His expertise prevented me from losing my important data and wasting money. David was an ANGEL.

My Answer Came Thru The Television   (5-1-2006)

Let me tell you about another time when I felt like God was hearing and answering my prayer, no matter how small it was.   A friend challenged me to solve a riddle about "thinking outside the box".   The challenge was to draw four straight lines which go through the middle of nine dots arranged in a set of three rows, without lifting the pencil/pen off the paper. As I was racking my brain trying to figure out the answer, I was watching a television investigation show that night, and then I heard the episode start asking exactly the same question! I was stunned that God had blessed little ole me with the answer, even through the television!   There was an ANGEL there somewhere. You've got to think outside the box in order to solve that one.

By the way, here's how you connect the nine dots for example: (1) Start at the top left dot and draw line-1 diagonally down through the middle dot to the bottom right dot. (2) Draw line-2 horizontally through the two left dots but continue onward the length of another invisible dot (outside of the box). (3) Draw line-3 diagonally from that invisible dot upward through the left middle dot and through the top middle dot for the length of a second invisible dot at the top right (outside the box). (4) Draw line-4 straight down to the bottom right dot. The finished product will look like an umbrella laid on its right side.

20th Year Anniversary Donations (5-20-2006)

In order to celebrate our QTMC 20-Year Anniversary we planned to host a picnic on our parking lot that day, and a big banquet dinner that night. Since we were a novice at hosting big picnics, I decided to talk with a man I know named Roger for advice, who has hosted a similar back-to-school picnic annually for years. I was extremely surprised that he not only offered advice, but he offered tents, games, food, and supplies. We were overwhelmed that he had gone far over and beyond the call of duty. Roger truly is an ANGEL.

Also, despite several family and friends making sincere commitments to donate their services for the picnic, before I knew it, I had about (100) people looking at me for the picnic food that I had promised, and I didn't even have a cook yet. Then up walked this young lady named Ladessa, who said that she would cook the hotdogs and hamburgers for me. She took control and organized the whole buffet line of food! Ladessa was an ANGEL.

Roofer Sleeping On My Porch   (7-1-2006)

In the summer of 2006, my son Steve's roof was leaking during every rain, and being the good Dad, I was determined to patch it up somehow. So I had purchased the ladder, materials and tools to get on the roof and fix it. It was a hot, punishing job, and after just one tough day, both of my day-laborers called it quits. So the next morning, I was very concerned because I didn't know how I was going to handle my unfinished project. Having grown spiritually into a lifestyle of expecting miracles, blessings, and ANGELS everyday, thru faith my specific prayer to God the previous night had been that "I need an ANGEL." The next morning, there was a homeless man sleeping outside the door of my building, so I asked him what he was up to. His name was Darryl, and I was in total surprise and disbelief for the rest of that day when the man informed me that he was a roofer looking for a job at the Labor Ready store across the street, but that they were closed, so he had stopped on my porch to rest since our reputation was that our shelter offered open arms to everyone down on their luck. I had summoned up an ANGEL with my faith, and God not only sent me an ANGEL, but He sent me a **qualified** ANGEL, who helped me install roof shingles on Steve's roof and then on my home also a year later. Darryl was an ANGEL.

Two Hundred T-Shirts (7-10-2006)

Whenever QTMC performs a youth concert, we usually throw a few t-shirts into the crowd of students to keep them pumped up. So we're always in search of a sponsor to provide a quantity of t-shirts. After we performed at the annual youth event on Belle Isle attended by 15,000 students, we contacted the organizers Ed and Keith to inquire if they had any surplus shirts. So they donated (200) t-shirts to us which we donate on to students as we perform motivational youth concerts in Detroit schools. They really helped replenish our stock of t-shirts so that we can always deliver a high-tempo concert. Ed and Keith were ANGELS.

An Unlikely Angel   (8-1-2006)

As a CHARITY, people frequently donate clothes, furniture, food, and finances to our cause. A donor had called me to come and pick up some furniture, and my sons and all my usual day-laborers that I was familiar with were busy, so I knew that I needed to find someone else in order to take some manpower with me. Expecting blessings everyday, I got off the phone and went outside the building looking for an ANGEL. Sure enough, there was a fellow named Luke sitting on my sidewalk beside the building. I had not seen Luke in about a year, but there he was, seemingly like from out of nowhere. As if God knew exactly who I needed, he had sent me a strong, muscle-bound ANGEL who lifted all the heavy furniture. Luke was unexpectedly sober that day, so therefore I realized that God may order the steps of anybody, at anytime, anywhere, in order to be an ANGEL in order to accomplish His will. Luke was an unlikely ANGEL.

Low Tire Pressure Almost Disastrous   (9-1-2006)

Another time we were driving to North Carolina in the Montana Van, and we had really loaded it down with luggage as well as our music equipment for the Romp-N-Stomp where we were headed. Steve was driving at that time. I could tell that the van was swaying all over the road, and not driving properly. I kept kidding myself that perhaps it would improve, but by the time that we had driven as far as Westland, Michigan, I decided that we were simply driving too dangerously on the expressway and we still had an 11-hour drive ahead of us. Being about 11:00pm at night, I began calling around for a wrecker company so that I could perhaps drive to them and get them to put the Van up on a shop jack in order to raise it up and examine the front end to diagnose the problem. When we arrived at the wrecker company, there were two men there. The older man seemed to be the boss, and he seemed set in his ways that he was not too concerned about helping a Minority family at that time of night, no matter how desperate we sounded. With our Christian light shining brightly through, nevertheless, he conceded and allowed the younger tow truck operator to check out the van. The young man went on a test drive with us to determine the problem, and he immediately mentioned that we need air in the tires. It was cold at night, so we stopped at a gas station and he put air in the tires. Unbelievable! The Van began to drive like new. Being a mechanic myself, mentally I was kicking myself for not having driven and diagnosed the problem myself. I had been trying to sleep while Steve began the kick-off driving. My family had been hearing me comment many times that whenever someone helped us thru a crisis situation, that perhaps they were an ANGEL, and that one day I was going to write a book about it. So after that incident, for the balance of that trip, my family was persistent that I should not delay any longer. **That incident persuaded me to finally start writing this very book**, so I began to write down many of the times that I recollected I may have seen an ANGEL. That young wrecker operator probably prevented us from having a flat tire on the expressway, as well as possible injury/death that night. We thanked God for him. He was an ANGEL.

Parade Vehicles Good Samaritan   (12-1-2006)

Almost every year for the last (22) years, QTMC / CENTERSTAGE has always participated in the annual Christmas Parade in our hometown. It's a tradition that we always enjoy. For 2006, I called the organizers as usual to receive our place number in the parade, and was introduced to a nice lady named Linda. After Linda gave me the number, she remarked that things were not going smoothly because the next day would be the parade, yet my employer General Motors had not furnished the expected (6) vehicles to tow the floats. So I said that although I was essentially a "nobody", I would still make a few calls to see what could be done. With my ever-present faith, I called one person, who led me to another person, who led me to the person who could make it happen. So before we knew it,

1. We had received commitment for (6) vehicles from the local General Motors dealer.
2. We had insurance placed on the vehicles.
3. We had signs created to put the dealer's logo on each vehicle.
4. We purchased tow-hooks for the trucks to pull the floats.
5. We designated the drivers for the vehicles.
6. We picked up the vehicles from the dealership.
7. We put gasoline in the vehicles.
8. We washed the vehicles.
9. We prominently displayed the vehicles in the parade.
10. We returned the vehicles back to the dealership.

I did not get an opportunity to breathe an unencumbered breath for two days. Needless to say, Linda was extremely grateful for my last-minute intervention. She even had a plaque made, and presented me with the ANGEL AWARD at the Parade Planning Committee meeting. I guess I really was her ANGEL for that day.

Right On Time (1-27-2007)

Since Steve took over the helm as sole rapper for QTMC Music Group (22) years ago, he has tirelessly represented at every performance concert that we've ever had, except for (3) concerts where "yours truly" had to be the lead rapper at Elementary Schools because the schools rejected any talk of cancellation. There have been (20) different QTMC Dancers whose careers we have helped launch, but they have gone on to pursue other careers. So we have always been looking for a replacement Rapper and Dancers. When Steve received the fantastic opportunity to be the Announcer for world famous The Harlem Globetrotters, we really began to search in earnest for another lead Rapper, because I already had about (20) confirmed bookings that it would have been difficult to cancel. So we advertised on our website, promoted word-of-mouth, passed out flyers, made announcements during concerts, and finally, held a full Saturday of auditions but **nobody** came. My hopes fell, and my faith wavered slightly as I contemplated my approach to call and cancel all of the upcoming concerts. But the very day that Steve had headed to Detroit to catch his plane to Phoenix, Arizona to begin The Harlem Globetrotters tour, a young man named Brian called Steve and me. He said that he had heard our CD from his Mom who got a copy when we had performed at the school where she worked, and wanted us to hear the gospel song that he had just created, hopeful that we could help promote airplay of his CD. I told him that he might be calling "right on time". He came to meet with me a few days later, and I gave him a copy of our QTMC performance track instrumental, plus a copy of the lyrics to the concert songs. He went home and quickly memorized them, and came back the next week ready to do a concert. So that cinched it for me that he possessed the qualifications necessary to temporarily perform in Steve's stead: motivation and self initiative, flexible schedule, stage presence, respect for following my lead, talent, looks, no foul language, and charisma. So take note that although we had been looking for someone like him for years, God waited until what seemed like the very last minute before sending someone, matter-of-fact someone with **exactly** the right skills for what

206

we needed. He came on the scene and helped maintain continuity of QTMC concerts, preventing concert cancellations for (2) years. Without him, I would have had to cancel about (20) concerts, and would have been prevented from continuing to book new concerts as event coordinators contacted me. Brian was an ANGEL.

Angels Carried Me On Their Wings   (3-2-2007)

March 2, 2007 was the most horrible night of my life. I had rented out our hall for a teen dance after the Pontiac Central versus Pontiac Northern High School basketball game. My contract with the renter required "tight" security, because of these two rival high schools in town. He lied. I didn't arrive at my building until about 11:00 pm, and there was only one security guard, and several guys were fighting him and getting the better of him. I corralled several of them and pushed them back so the security guard got up off the floor. Then, I rushed over to my front entryway to check on the commotion there. When I got there, I told this teenager to stop trying to break out my front door glass. That was the last thing that I saw for two days. One teen tackled me from behind, out my door onto the pavement outside. Then, with a mob mentality, (8) high school teenagers kicked me in the head, face, and eyes mercilessly. Before I was kicked unconscious, I heard some girls' voices saying "y'all leave that man alone!!" several times before the attack stopped, as they left me for dead. I had been cruelly beaten just short of death. I was unconscious, bloody, and blind from my eyes being kicked shut. I remember the girls carried me inside and laid me down on the floor in my pool of blood until the ambulance came. My eyes were swollen shut for two days, and the white parts of my eyes were blood red so I had to miss work to recuperate for a month due to my head and neck injuries. To this day I still have nerve damage and loss of some sensation in my left arm. When the attack appeared in the local newspaper that next week, outraged students began to call and give the names of my attempted assassins. I received about (10) phone calls, all naming the same (8) high school seniors who had attacked me unprovoked. But despite numerous attempts by me to demand a meeting with the young men and their parents, plus a fiery letter that I sent to, and a meeting that I attended with, the Mayor and Chief of Police, no action was ever taken whatsoever. It took all that I could do to stop my sons or my homeless friends from seeking vigilante justice on those young men. I thank God for keeping me alive, so I resolved to "Let Go, and Let God". If those girls had not stopped the attack when they did, then I may not have survived. If the question was to be asked "why did God let a bad thing happen to a good person, having experienced it, I would answer "so that the name of God would be exalted and praised, and in order to humble hundreds of people to be praying to Him without ceasing for my recovery", because that was the ultimate result of that attack. With an attitude of gratitude, I shall always praise Him anyway. Hallelujah! Those girls were my ANGELS.

Jack Needs An Angel   (8-1-2007)

Another time, I was helping my friend Jack move some furniture, and we had a heavy sofa to carry down some stairs, and I could handle my end, but Jack had a weak back which prevented him from lifting anything too heavy. I told him "We need an ANGEL, so I'm going to go and get us an ANGEL". I went outside and glanced around the neighborhood, but there were no likely prospects to be seen. So we moved the rest of the light weight furniture instead, then we came back to the problem of the heavy furniture. Again, I went outside to look around, and noticed Jack's next door neighbor named Stephen driving into the driveway. By the time that he had gotten out of his car, I had approached him and I told him that he may not know it yet, but I had been expecting him. He was strong enough to help me carry that heavy sofa down the stairs and loaded it into my truck. Stephen was an ANGEL.

Broken Kitchen Light Switch   (8-5-2007)

The CENTERSTAGE was hosting the entire medical class from a Michigan university to set up an actual "M.A.S.H." unit hospital and operate on dozens of animals, and as I scurried around trying to make sure that everything was going okay for my customer, I noticed that my lights wouldn't come on in the kitchen. You know the old Murphy's Law cliché, "whatever can go wrong, will" (and at the wrong time I might add). Despite my best efforts, I simply could not get those lights to come on! Then, one of the animal care volunteers named Keith who had just arrived saw my plight and offered his assistance. Seems like he came from nowhere! Turns out that Keith was an electrician. He analyzed the problem, drove to the hardware store and purchased a light switch, and came back and installed it. He came out of nowhere and rescued me from a desperate situation. Again, God knew exactly who I needed, so he sent me a **qualified** ANGEL. Keith was an ANGEL.

Storms In The Area   (5-30-2008)

In order to provide temporary warming facilities for the homeless/needy community during the wintry season from Thanksgiving to Easter for the last 12 years, besides the thousands of meals that we've served, inherently there are astronomical utility bills such as electrical bill, heating bill, and water bill. Through faith, sacrifices from my own finances, donations from contributors, and payment plan arrangements, I usually always stay one step ahead of a dreaded utility shutoff. When I missed the electrical bill payment plan arrangement though, the Electric Company cut off the electricity at our rental hall building. With a customer's Wedding Reception coming in a few days, I was in crisis mode as I borrowed some money to add to mine in order to pay the overdue bill. After I had paid the bill on that Friday, then the Electric Company lady told me the disappointing news that they could not schedule anyone to turn the electricity back on until the next week. Then, I really panicked and began about 20-minutes of begging, pleading, cajoling, begging, imploring, enticing, begging, persuading, soliciting, begging (did I say this one before?) for Electric Company to cut my electricity back on so that we could host the Wedding Reception. But it was all to no avail, so my hopes fell in desperation as I resolved to the fact that I was now in more trouble with the looming Wedding Reception. After I left work in Detroit and commuted back to Pontiac that evening, I went to the building to check on things, and was shocked to see that the electricity was turned back on! I saw a few of my homeless friends outside on my parking lot, so I asked them did they see the Electric Company man cut the lights back on. They said that the man who climbed the post to turn on the electricity had said that due to **storms in the area**, that Electric Company was being proactive by positioning scores of trucks in the area, so that they could immediately respond to any service call. So although the Electric Company lady was adamant for 20 minutes that she could not dispatch a person for (4) days to cut the lights back on, they were cut back on within (4) hours! I was astounded! I was thinking to myself about what a mighty God that I serve! He knew what I needed so he had uniquely

212

positioned a **fleet** of trucks waiting to serve me. That Electric Company man who climbed the post and cut on the electricity was an ANGEL.

Free Toys, Free Coats   (12-18-2008)

Our small CHARITY has been gaining in popularity over the years, and nowadays, it seems like we receive clothes, furniture, toys, coats, and financial contributions almost at the same pace as the Salvation Army. With the stuff that we receive, we always endeavor to donate it on to homeless persons or needy families, the intended recipients. In order to let people know that we have something available to donate to the community, we decided to put a notification on our roadside billboard sign in front of our rental hall building. The manager named Andria of a local restaurant in Pontiac, called us one day to advise that she was going to be hosting a fundraiser for us, so we made our plans to attend. She was very kind and cheerful, shunning the limelight as we tried to give her props on the microphone that night for her dedication. She even personally made some scarves, necklaces, pocketbooks, and other wares which were sold for the fundraiser. It was a very memorable and fruitful night of raising many canned goods and donations, with part of the proceeds going to our CHARITY. We thanked Andria for hosting this unprecedented fundraiser for us, and I inquired as to what gave her the idea to help us. We were surprised that she said that a year earlier, as she drove past our billboard that displayed "Free Toys", and even during the fundraiser was then showing "Free Coats", that she had decided that such kindness of giving from the heart should be rewarded. Wow! From what I thought was an insignificant action of putting "Free Toys" on a billboard a year ago, a total stranger had decided to host a fundraiser for us at her restaurant. Wow! That was so sweet, kind, and generous of her. Andria is an ANGEL.

214

Thanksgiving Feed The Homeless/Needy Program

As a Co-Partner in QTMC, Inc. and CENTERSTAGE Rental Hall, I realized my "calling" when we began hosting annual Thanksgiving Feed/Clothe/Shelter the Homeless/Needy Programs each winter. Although spearheaded by me, frequently the rest of my family also assists in this monumental task with transportation and serving of meals as necessary.

Thanksgiving 1997 is when the word ANGEL became more of a regular part of my environment. At the CENTERSTAGE Rental Hall that my family and I operate, we hosted our 1St Annual Thanksgiving Feed / Clothe / Shelter the Homeless / Needy Program. As the brand new owners, we were compelled to act because we read that: Luke 14:12-13 **Jesus** said *"When thou makest a dinner or a supper, call not thy friends, nor thy brethren, neither thy kinsmen, nor thy rich neighbors, but when thou makest a feast, call the poor, the maimed, the lame, and the blind. And thou shalt be blessed."*

My personal mission statement that I've adopted since then is to "Live my life in such a way that people who know me, but don't know Christ, will come to know Christ because they know me." I try to treat everyone with the utmost compassion, respect, and dignity, so that people will see Christ exemplified in my life and glorify the Father in Heaven. Thanksgiving 2008 was our 12th Annual Thanksgiving Program, and as you can imagine, I have been called an ANGEL so often for helping less fortunate people that even I started to believe it myself. It has made me acutely aware that we all need to strive to be His humble servant at all times in order to always be worthy to be used by Him to do His will. Our Thanksgiving experience has caused me to notice even more, other ANGELS in our lives who strive to do God's will, and has provided ample opportunities for many Volunteers to "earn their wings" and many ANGELS to reveal themselves such as:

215

(11-23-2000) When we had first begun to provide temporary warming refuge, Cindy had donated some boxes of emergency blankets, which we exhausted that supply by the next winter. Being a 501c3 nonprofit QTMC, Inc. Charity, I placed an order with the federal government for blankets to replenish my depleted stock. I ordered sixty (60) blankets, but they sent me (200) emergency blankets. These are thick, wool, best-quality, emergency blankets that we provide to each homeless person who receives temporary warming and refuge at our CENTERSTAGE. She had alleviated the major concern that I had regarding securing those necessary blankets. Cindy was an ANGEL.

(11-22-2001) Two husband and wife duos named Rick & Lesa and Charles & Loretta had brought some food from their catering company in Clarkston to a local Pontiac community to hopefully serve the homeless, but there was hardly anyone around because it was so cold outside. So they came to the CENTERSTAGE and donated (50) hot, complete Thanksgiving meals to us that day. At the time that they came, I was just starting to run short of several foods, so they were really right on time. Rick & Lesa and Charles & Loretta were ANGELS.

(11-26-2003) The Pastor of a church had also received some food to serve the community, and then he learned of our Thanksgiving meal being prepared, so he donated (180) apple and cherry pies. We refrigerated some of them, and they lasted all winter, and plus we donated some of them to needy families in the community. That Pastor was an ANGEL.

(11-30-2003) There is a lady named Kirklin who worked at a grocery store which specializes in organic foods. Therefore, without preservatives and such, each week the store has a lot of potential spoilage of meats, vegetables, fruit, and juices. Kirklin put us on the schedule for food donations each week during winter, and that's when the word "bountiful" became a regular part of my vocabulary. She ensured that our Feed The Homeless program usually had a bountiful portion of all that we needed to feed the multitudes. Kirklin was an ANGEL.

(11-24-2004) Our rental hall has (4) restrooms, and we provide temporary warming shelter from about 5:30 am to 8:30pm for about (100) men and women every Saturday and Sunday from Thanksgiving to Easter for the last (12) years. As a consequence, paper products are a challenge to keep in stock. One of our contributors named Nancy became aware of this matter, and remembered that her company was switching to new style dispensers for their bathrooms, so they were throwing all of the old style away. They authorized me to pick up all of the discarded obsolete stock at their loading dock, so I loaded up my Suburban's eight feet of cargo space to the maximum limit on three different trips with about (2,000) rolls of toilet paper stuffed into large plastic bags. When I put all of the bags into my storage room at the CENTERSTAGE, they touched the ceiling! That supply alleviated my toilet paper expense for three years. Nancy was an ANGEL.

(11-17-2006) Our QTMC Music Group performed at a metro Detroit High School one Friday night, at an event billed as "Safe Night". How ironic, that some students started a fight, and the event had to be abruptly cancelled. Knowing our involvement with feeding the homeless/needy, rather than waste all of the snacks, the organizer Chris therefore donated (200) bags of potato chips and about (20) 2-liter bottles of soda pop to us. That really supplemented our Thanksgiving meal that next week. Chris was an ANGEL.

(1-20-2007) A Father of a local Parish of churches has donated food, clothing, and shelter, as well as provided hot nutritious meals to homeless/needy community families many times. He also donated use of his facilities for us to host the 2007 Christmas Feed the Homeless/Needy Meals event in his church gymnasium. Also, whenever my rental hall was rented out to a revenue producing customer, thereby preventing me from hosting the homeless community for that particular cold winter day, the Father graciously provided his facilities at no-charge. Several times, whenever he had hosted an event at one of his churches, but there was food left over, he donated it to us

217

for us to serve it to the homeless/needy. That Father was an ANGEL.

(12-8-2007) A lady named Tammi and her family volunteered one time, and therefore took notice of several items that we were in dire need of. Subsequently, they came back with new electric can openers, food, and many paper products. Also, Tammi sacrificed her own Christmas present from her family, and donated her new deep frying pan to us! Tammi was an ANGEL.

(12-25-2007) For Christmas 2007, I was approached by a nice lady named Jacqueline, who asked me to use my resources and other sources to join forces with her to host Christmas Feed the Homeless/Needy Meals. She wanted to continue a tradition that she had previously been carrying on with her mentor called "Mother". Having just completed our exhaustive Thanksgiving program, I knew that we had to try something new in order to bring our dream to fruition, so I wrote a letter to the Pontiac Food Bank asking for food assistance. We were overwhelmed when they donated two pallet-loads of canned goods plus about ten cases of soda pop. We were bountifully blessed so much so that we did not have room enough to receive it. My cup overfloweth with blessings, and I need a bigger cup, so I live every day expecting God to bless me with a bigger one. In addition to serving everyone bountifully all winter from our new storehouse, we have sought needy families in the community and allowed them to go shopping in our pantry at the CENTERSTAGE. My shelves are not empty yet, and it seems like they never will be as long as we remain committed to serving others as we strive to remain God's humble servants. Since I met Jacqueline, she has cheerfully donated her time and talents, and enlisted several of her friends and family, to help me cook and serve the homeless/needy community on many occasions. Jacqueline is an ANGEL.

(12-28-2007) Each winter kickoff, we are always overwhelmed by the large numbers of volunteers. It's always overcrowded in our little ole kitchen, but we don't want to deny anyone an opportunity to earn their wings, so I always let potential volunteers know that we expect to be crowded, so it is their prerogative if they should elect to volunteer.   Whole families, as well as various churches, come to help us serve Thanksgiving meals each year. That's how I met Toni and Joanne. They're two ladies who jumped in with both feet. In addition to serving as volunteers during the kickoff, they have since returned on about four other occasions to bring donations of food, meats, money, and several boxes of pots and pans! They're from a church in Farmington Hills, and began a grassroots effort and obtained donations from several of their fellow parishioners. They have really been a huge blessing to us. Toni and Joanne are ANGELS.

(1-26-2008) Another person who goes above and beyond the call of duty is a man named Pastor Kevin who started helping from a church in Clarkston.   After volunteering at the Thanksgiving kickoff, Pastor Kevin recognized our needs, and returned in full force a few weeks later with about (80) people from his church. They showered our little Feed The Homeless ministry with an over-abundance of various foods, a new microwave oven and kitchen stove, and financial gifts. They really, really, overfilled our cup, so that we hardly had room enough to receive it.   Our refrigerators, freezers, and cupboards were overflowing. Pastor Kevin is an ANGEL.

I WROTE A SONG FOR ANGELS

As the Manager of QTMC Music Group over the last 30 years, I have written and copyrighted about 50 songs. I wrote the next song for ANGELS, "A Standing Ovation". There are several groups of people that I feel do not receive the just recognition or reward due to them. During any school assembly or other special event, students should recite this poem with a special Teacher, Parent, Policeman, Fireman, or Soldier. Many of them are ANGELS.

Teachers, Parents, Policemen, Firemen, & Soldiers Deserve "A Standing Ovation"

Special Teacher, Parent, Policeman, Fireman Or Soldier:

The persons to be honored are our heroes and friends.
They've taught us the right values from beginning to end.
Encouraging us to soar like an eagle in everything,
They're our Teachers, Parents, Policemen, Firemen, &
Soldiers: The wind beneath our wings.

You've reminded us that in order to achieve,
We must believe,
In the power of education, and the passion to read.
Teaching with fairness and determination,
You diligently serve with hope and dedication.

You taught us to approach life with positive visions,
With motivation and education to make the right decisions.
You taught us that our potential is within reach,
That we're only limited by our courage to seek.

You've encouraged us to be responsible youth,
That we'll only win when we embrace the truth.
Our success in life will only be measured,
By the values and respect you've taught us to treasure.
You taught us that, at whatever we strive to be,
Or whatever we may one day decide to be,
Don't be a menace to society,

220

But do it with all of our might sincerely.
Challenging situations bring out the best in you.
But you always look for the positive view,
For all the drama that we bring from home,
Sometimes taking you from your comfort zone.
Being a good leader is always emphasized.
You've made a real difference in each of our lives.
Whether academic skills or curriculum course,
Your guidance helps us to make the right choice.

You've touched our hearts in a very special way.
You've been there for us each learning day,
Giving us instruction to prevent our destruction,
And giving us correction to guide us in the right direction.
You're a gracious role model always offer friendly advice.
Sharing your time unselfishly, that's your sacrifice.
With love and devotion to help others, you expect no award,
Cheering for your students to succeed is your main reward.

Memories may fade from the lessons you've taught.
But we'll always remember your kind actions and thoughts.
We'll always remember the joy that you've made us feel.
You've made us feel important, and we thank you sincerely.

Students don't say it enough, and it may not show,
But we appreciate you much more than you know.
You're a winner, a champion, a friend, and a hero.
We admire you; we're inspired by you, to set higher goals.

You're someone special,
And the reason why we reach for the sky.
You're a positive influence, and a part of our life.
Your well-deserved recognition is long overdue,
Teachers, Parents, Policemen, Firemen, & Soldiers:
We salute you.

We gratefully thank you for your worthy cause.
Our tribute to you: we stand in your honor,
We give you applause,
We ask students to join us all over the nation.
Teachers, Parents, Policemen, Firemen, & Soldiers:
Deserve *"A STANDING OVATION"*.

THE END

I hereby affirm that everything in this book is genuine, accurate, and true to the best of my ability. I'm Dave Coleman, a normal person striving to be God's most humble servant, and I approve this book.

222

Printed in the United States
Bookmasters.

Printed in the United States
By Bookmasters